Vivekachudamani

Also available from Evertype

Ashtavakra Gita: The Heart of Awareness
(Attrib. Aṣṭāvakra, tr. John Richards 2019)

De Adhaerendo Deo: On Cleaving to God (Attributed to Albertus Magnus, written by Johannes von Kastl, tr. John Richards 2022)

The Dhammapada: The Sayings of the Buddha
(Tr. Ānandajoti Bhikku 2019)

George Fox: A Christian Mystic
(By Hugh McGregor Ross 2008)

Get a grip and stay sane: Self-Healing with the Nadi Technique
(By Billy Roberts 2016)

The Idyll of the White Logus and The Story of Sensa
(By Mabel Collins 2022)

Ifflepinn Island: A tale to read aloud for greengrowing children and evergreen adults
(Written and illustrated by Muz Murray 2014)

The Prophet
(Written and illustrated by Kahlil Gibran 2019)

Thirty Essays on the Gospel of Thomas
(By Hugh McGregor Ross 2008)

Vivekachudamani: The Crest-Jewel of Discrimination
(Attrib. Adi Shankara, tr. John Richards 2022)

What thou wilt: Traditional and Innovative Trends in Post-Garnerian Witchcraft
(By Jon Hanna 2010)

Vivekachudamani

The Crest-Jewel of Discrimination

A bilingual edition in Sanskrit and English

Attributed to
Adi Shankara

Transcribed and translated by
John Richards

evertype
2022

Published by Evertype, 19A Corso Street, Dundee, DD2 1DR, Scotland. www.evertype.com.

Editor: Michael Everson.

A catalogue record for this book is available from the British Library.

ISBN-10 1-78201-169-2
ISBN-13 978-1-78201-169-9

Typeset in Baskerville and New Pelican by Michael Everson.

Design and cover design: Michael Everson. "Mandala retro background" © Annagarmatiy, www.dreamstime.com/annagarmatiy_info.

Preface

The Reverend John Henry Richards, ma, bd, was an Anglican priest born in 1934 who was ordained a deacon in Llandaff in 1977 and a priest there in 1978. He served in Maesteg, Cardiff, Penmark, and Stackpile Elidor until his retirement in 1999, and died in 2017. He is known for his English translations of the Sanskrit *Ashtavakra Gita* and *Vivekachudamani*, of the Pali *Dhammapada*, and of the medieval Latin *De Adhærendo Deo*, all of which he put in the public domain and distributed on the Internet in the late 1990s.

I have made a very few alterations to John's text and translation, replacing the Devanagari daṇḍa and double daṇḍa with the vertical bar and double vertical bar surrounding the verse numbers in the Sanskrit text, adding "said" to correspond to *uvāca* to introduce the dialogue in the translation, and favouring Oxford spelling.

A table of contents has been given listing the verses in groups of about 50; this sort of grouping isn't relevant to the content of the work, but is found in many editions, so it has been added here. Verse ranges for each page are given in the header.

Michael Everson
Dundee, April 2022

Vivekachudamani

Anukramaṇikā

Ślokāḥ 1–52 4
Ślokāḥ 53–106 16
Ślokāḥ 107–156 28
Ślokāḥ 157–199 30
Ślokāḥ 200–251 50
Ślokāḥ 252–303 62
Ślokāḥ 304–352 74
Ślokāḥ 353–401 86
Ślokāḥ 402–448 98
Ślokāḥ 449–503 108
Ślokāḥ 504–554 120
Ślokāḥ 555–580 132

Table of Contents

Verses 1–52 5
Verses 53–106 17
Verses 107–156 29
Verses 157–199 31
Verses 200–251 51
Verses 252–303 63
Verses 304–352 75
Verses 353–401 87
Verses 402–448 99
Verses 449–503 109
Verses 504–554 121
Verses 555–580 133

A Note on the Text 138

Vivekacūḍāmaṇi

sarvavedāntasiddhāntagocaraṃ tamagocaram |
govindaṃ paramānandaṃ sadguruṃ praṇato'smyaham || 1 ||

jantūnāṃ narajanma durlabhamataḥ puṃstvaṃ tato vipratā
tasmādvaidikadharmamārgaparatā vidvattvamasmātparam |
ātmānātmavivecanaṃ svanubhavo brahmātmanā saṃsthitiḥ
muktirno śatajanmakoṭisukṛtaiḥ puṇyairvinā labhyate || 2 ||

durlabhaṃ trayamevaitaddevānugrahahetukam |
manuṣyatvaṃ mumukṣutvaṃ mahāpuruṣasaṃśrayaḥ || 3 ||

labdhvā kathaṃcinnarajanma durlabhaṃ
tatrāpi puṃstvaṃ śrutipāradarśanam |
yastvātmamuktau na yateta mūḍhadhīḥ
sa hyātmahā svaṃ vinihantyasadgrahāt || 4 ||

itaḥ ko nvasti mūḍhātmā yastu svārthe pramādyati |
durlabhaṃ mānuṣaṃ dehaṃ prāpya tatrāpi pauruṣam || 5 ||

vadantu śāstrāṇi yajantu devān
kurvantu karmāṇi bhajantu devatāḥ |
ātmaikyabodhena vināpi muktiḥ
na sidhyati brahmaśatāntare'pi || 6 ||

Vivekachudamani
Crest-Jewel of Discrimination

1 I prostrate myself before Govinda, the true Guru and ultimate Bliss, who is the unattainable resort of all scriptures and Vedanta.

2 Human nature is the hardest of creaturely states to obtain, even more so that of manhood. Brahminhood is rarer still, and beyond that dedication to the path of Vedic religion. Beyond even that there is discrimination between self and non-self, but liberation by persistence in the state of the unity of God and self is not to be achieved except by the meritorious deeds of hundreds of thousands of lives.

3 These three things are hard to achieve, and are attained only by the grace of God—human nature, the desire for liberation, and finding refuge with a great sage.

4 He is a suicide who has somehow achieved human birth and even manhood and full knowledge of the scriptures but does not strive for self-liberation, for he destroys himself by clinging to the unreal.

5 Who could be more foolish than the man who has achieved the difficult attainment of a human body and even manhood but still neglects his true good?

6 People may quote the scriptures, make sacrifices to the gods, perform actions and pay homage to the deities, but there is no liberation without recognizing the oneness of one's own true being—not even in the lifetime of a hundred Brahmas.[1]

---

1 countless millions of years.

amṛtatvasya nāśāsti vittenetyeva hi śrutiḥ |
bravīti karmaṇo mukterahetutvaṃ sphuṭaṃ yataḥ || 7 ||

ato vimuktyai prayatetvidvān
saṃnyastabāhyārthasukhaspṛhaḥ san |
santaṃ mahāntaṃ samupetya deśikaṃ
tenopadiṣṭārthasamāhitātmā || 8 ||

uddharedātmanātmānaṃ magnaṃ saṃsāravāridhau |
yogārūḍhatvamāsādya samyagdarśananiṣṭhayā || 9 ||

saṃnyasya sarvakarmāṇi bhavabandhavimuktaye |
yatyatāṃ paṇḍitairdhīrairātmābhyāsa upasthitaiḥ || 10 ||

cittasya śuddhaye karma na tu vastūpalabdhaye |
vastusiddhirvicāreṇa na kiṃcitkarmakoṭibhiḥ || 11 ||

samyagvicārataḥ siddhā rajjutattvāvadhāraṇā |
bhrāntoditamahāsarpabhayaduḥkhavināśinī || 12 ||

arthasya niścayo dṛṣṭo vicāreṇa hitoktitaḥ |
na snānena na dānena prāṇāyamaśatena vā || 13 ||

adhikāriṇamāśāste phalasiddhirviśeṣataḥ |
upāyā deśakālādyāḥ santyasminsahakāriṇaḥ || 14 ||

ato vicāraḥ kartavyo jijñāsorātmavastunaḥ |
samāsādya dayāsindhuṃ guruṃ brahmaviduttamam || 15 ||

medhāvī puruṣo vidvānuhāpohavicakṣaṇaḥ |
adhikāryātmavidyāyāmuktalakṣaṇalakṣitaḥ || 16 ||

7 Scripture declares that there is no hope of immortality by means of wealth, so it is evident that liberation cannot be brought about by actions.

8 So let the man of understanding strive for liberation, abandoning desire for the enjoyment of external aims and pleasures, and after becoming the pupil of a good and great teacher, let him fix his mind on the goal he indicates.

9 Sunk in the sea of samsara, one should oneself rouse oneself by holding onto right understanding until one reaches the state of the attainment of union.

10 Abandoning all actions and breaking free from the bonds of achievements, the wise and intelligent should apply themselves to self-knowledge.

11 Action is for the purification of the mind, not for the understanding of reality. The recognition of reality is through discrimination, and not by even tens of millions of actions.

12 Proper analysis leads to the realization of the reality of the rope, and this is the end of the pain of the fear of the great snake caused by delusion.

13 The realization of the truth is seen to depend on meditation on statements about what is good, not on bathing or donations or by hundreds of yogic breathing exercises.

14 Achievement of the goal depends primarily on a fit seeker. Things like locality and time are merely secondary in this matter.

15 So he who would know his own nature should practise meditation on the subject after taking refuge with a guru who is a true knower of God and an ocean of compassion.

16 It is the wise and learned man, skilled in sorting out the pros and cons of an argument who is really endowed with the qualities necessary for self-realization.

vivekino viraktasya śamādiguṇaśālinaḥ |
mumukṣoreva hi brahmajijñāsāyogyatā matā || 17 ||

sādhanānyatra catvāri kathitāni manīṣibhiḥ |
yeṣu satsveva sanniṣṭhā yadabhāve na sidhyati || 18 ||

ādau nityānityavastuvivekaḥ parigamyate |
ihāmutraphalabhogavirāgastadanantaram
śamādiṣaṭkasampattirmumukṣutvamiti sphuṭam || 19 ||

brahma satyaṃ jaganmithyetyevaṃrūpo viniścayaḥ |
so'yaṃ nityānityavastuvivekaḥ samudāhṛtaḥ || 20 ||

tadvairāgyaṃ jihāsā yā darśanaśravaṇādibhiḥ |
dehādibrahmaparyante hyanitye bhogavastuni || 21 ||

virajya viṣayavrātāddoṣadṛṣṭyā muhurmuhuḥ |
svalakṣye niyatāvasthā manasaḥ śama ucyate || 22 ||

viṣayebhyaḥ parāvartya sthāpanaṃ svasvagolake |
ubhayeṣāmindriyāṇāṃ sa damaḥ parikīrtitaḥ
bāhyānālambanaṃ vṛttereṣoparatiruttamā || 23 ||

sahanaṃ sarvaduḥkhānāmapratīkārapūrvakam |
cintāvilāparahitaṃ sā titikṣā nigadyate || 24 ||

śāstrasya guruvākyasya satyabuddhyavadhāraṇam |
sā śraddhā kathitā sadbhiryayā vastūpalabhyate || 25 ||

sarvadā sthāpanaṃ buddheḥ śuddhe brahmaṇi sarvadā |
tatsamādhānamityuktaṃ na tu cittasya lālanam || 26 ||

17 Discriminating and dispassionate, endowed with peace and similar qualities, and longing for liberation—such is the man who is considered fit to practise seeking for God.

18 The wise talk here of four qualities, possessed of which one will succeed, but without which one will fail.

19 First is listed discrimination between unchanging and changing realities, and after that dispassion for the enjoyment of the fruits of action both here and hereafter, and then the group of six qualities including peace and of course the desire for liberation.

20 "God is the Truth and the world is unreal." It is this realization that is considered discrimination between the permanent and the impermanent.

21 Dispassion is the turning away from what can be seen and heard and so on in everything which is impermanent, from the body up to the highest heavenly states.

22 The settling of the mind in its goal, by turning away from the mass of objects through observing their defects again and again, is known as peace.

23 The establishment of the senses each in its own source by means of turning away from their objects is known as control. The supreme restraint is in the mind function not being involved in anything external.

24 Bearing all afflictions without retaliation and without mental disturbance is what is known as patience.

25 The holding on to the knowledge of the truth of the Scriptures and the guru's teaching is called faith. It is by means of this that reality is grasped.

26 The continual holding onto the awareness of God alone - continually, is known as concentration—not just mental self-gratification.

ahaṃkārādidehāntān bandhānajñānakalpitān |
svasvarūpāvabodhena moktumicchā mumukṣutā || 27 ||

mandamadhyamarūpāpi vairāgyeṇa śamādinā |
prasādena guroḥ seyaṃ pravṛddhā sūyate phalam || 28 ||

vairāgyaṃ ca mumukṣutvaṃ tīvraṃ yasya tu vidyate |
tasminnevārthavantaḥ syuḥ phalavantaḥ śamādayaḥ || 29 ||

etayormandatā yatra viraktatvamumukṣayoḥ |
marau salīlavattatra śamāderbhānamātratā || 30 ||

mokṣakāraṇasāmagryāṃ bhaktireva garīyasī |
svasvarūpānusandhānaṃ bhaktirityabhidhīyate || 31 ||

svātmatattvānusandhānaṃ bhaktirityapare jaguḥ |
uktasādhanasaṃpannastattvajijñāsurātmanaḥ
upasīdedguruṃ prājñyaṃ yasmādbandhavimokṣaṇam || 32 ||

śrotriyo'vṛjino'kāmahato yo brahmavittamaḥ |
brahmaṇyuparataḥ śānto nirindhana ivānalaḥ
ahetukadayāsindhurbandhurānamatāṃ satām || 33 ||

amārādhya guruṃ bhaktyā prahvapraśrayasevanaiḥ |
prasannaṃ tamanuprāpya pṛcchejjñātavyamātmanaḥ || 34 ||

svāminnamaste natalokabandho
kāruṇyasindho patitaṃ bhavābdhau |
māmuddharātmīyakaṭākṣadṛṣṭyā
ṛjvyātikāruṇyasudhābhivṛṣṭyā || 35 ||

27 The wish to be freed by the knowledge of one's true nature from such bonds as seeing oneself as the agent, which are contingent on the body and created by ignorance—this is desire for liberation.

28 This desire for liberation can bear fruit through dispassion, peacefulness etc. by the grace of the guru, even when only weak or mediocre.

29 It is in a man who has strong dispassion and desire for liberation though that peacefulness and so on are really fruitful.

30 But where there is a weakness in these qualities of renunciation and desire for liberation, apparent peacefulness and such like have as much substance as water in the desert.

31 Among the contributory factors of liberation, devotion stands supreme, and it is the search for one's own true nature that is meant by devotion.

32 Others say that devotion is inquiry into the reality of one's own nature. He who possesses the above qualities and would know the truth about his own nature should take refuge with a wise guru who can free him from his bonds.

33 The guru should be one who knows the scriptures, is blameless and a supreme knower of God. He should be at peace in God, tranquil as a fire that has run out of fuel. He should be a boundless ocean of compassion and the friend of those who seek his protection.

34 After prostrating oneself with devotion before the guru and satisfying him with prostrations, humble devotion and service, one should ask him what one needs to know.

35 Hail, lord, friend of those who bow before you, and ocean of compassion. I have fallen into this sea of samsara. Save me with a direct glance from your eye which bestows grace like nectar.

durvārasaṃsāradavāgnitaptaṃ
dodhūyamānaṃ duradṛṣṭavātaiḥ |
bhītaṃ prapannaṃ paripāhi mṛtyoḥ
śaraṇyamanyadyadahaṃ na jāne || 36 ||

śāntā mahānto nivasanti santo
vasantavallokahitaṃ carantaḥ |
tīrṇāḥ svayaṃ bhīmabhavārṇavaṃ janān
ahetunān yānapi tārayantaḥ || 37 ||

ayaṃ svabhāvaḥ svata eva yatpara
śramāpanodapravaṇaṃ mahātmanām |
sudhāṃśureṣa svayamarkakarkaśa
prabhābhitaptāmavati kṣitiṃ kila || 38 ||

rahmānandarasānubhūtikalitaiḥ pūrtaiḥ suśītairyutaiḥ
yuṣmadvākkalaśojjhitaiḥ śrutisukhairvākyāmṛtaiḥ secaya |
saṃtaptaṃ bhavatāpadāvadahanajvālābhirenaṃ prabho
dhanyāste bhavadīkṣaṇakṣaṇagateḥ pātrīkṛtāḥ svīkṛtāḥ || 39 ||

kathaṃ tareyaṃ bhavasindhumetaṃ
kā vā gatirme katamo'styupāyaḥ |
jāne na kiñjcitkṛpayāva māṃ prabho
saṃsāraduḥkhakṣatimātanuṣva || 40 ||

tathā vadantaṃ śaraṇāgataṃ svaṃ
saṃsāradāvānalatāpataptam |
nirīkṣya kāruṇyarasārdradṛṣṭyā
dadyādabhītiṃ sahasā mahātmā || 41 ||

vidvān sa tasmā upasattimīyuṣe
mumukṣave sādhu yathoktakāriṇe |
praśāntacittāya śamānvitāya
tattvopadeśaṃ kṛpayaiva kuryāt || 42 ||

mā bhaiṣṭa vidvaṃstava nāstyapāyaḥ
saṃsārasindhostaraṇe'styupāyaḥ |
yenaiva yātā yatayo'sya pāraṃ
tameva mārgaṃ tava nirdiśāmi || 43 ||

36 I am stricken by the unquenchable forest fire of samsara and blown about by unforeseeable winds of circumstances. Save me from death, for I am afraid and take refuge in you, for I know of no one else to help me.

37 Good and peaceful, great men living for the good of all, and having themselves crossed the fearful torrent of becoming, with no ulterior motive help others to cross too.

38 It is the nature of great souls to act spontaneously for the relief of the distress of others, just as the moon here of itself protects the earth parched by the heat of the fierce rays of the sun.

39 Pour upon me your sweet words, imbued with the taste of God's bliss. They spring from your lips as if poured out of a jug, and are pleasing to the ear. For I am tormented by samsara's afflictions, like the flames of a forest fire, Lord. Blessed are those who receive even a passing glance from your eyes.

40 How can I cross this sea of changing circumstances? What should I do, what means employ? In your mercy, Lord, show me how to end the pain of samsara, for I understand nothing.

41 As he said this, tormented by the forest fire of samsara, the great Sage looked at him with a gaze full of compassion, urging him to abandon fear, now that he had taken refuge in him.

42 Out of compassion the Sage undertakes his instruction since he has come to him for help in his search for liberation, is willing to do as he is told, is pacified of mind and calm.

43 Don't be afraid, master. Destruction is not for you. There is indeed a means of crossing the sea of samsara, the way taken by which those who have crossed over before, and I will now instruct you in it.

astyupāyo mahān kaścitsaṃsārabhayanāśanaḥ |
tena tīrtvā bhavāmbhodhiṃ paramānandamāpsyasi || 44 ||

vedāntārthavicāreṇa jāyate jñānamuttamam |
tenātyantikasaṃsāraduḥkhanāśo bhavatyanu || 45 ||

śraddhābhaktidhyānayogāmmumukṣoḥ
mukterhetūnvakti sākṣācchrutergīḥ |
yo vā eteṣveva tiṣṭhatyamuṣya
mokṣo'vidyākalpitāddehabandhāt || 46 ||

ajñānayogātparamātmanastava
hyanātmabandhastata eva saṃsṛtiḥ |
tayorvivekoditabodhavanhiḥ
ajñānakāryaṃ pradahetsamūlam || 47 ||

śiṣya uvāca ||

kṛpayā śrūyatāṃ svāmin praśno'yaṃ kriyate mayā |
yaduttaramahaṃ śrutvā kṛtārthaḥ syāṃ bhavanmukhāt || 48 ||

ko nāma bandhaḥ kathameṣa āgataḥ
kathaṃ pratiṣṭhāsya kathaṃ vimokṣaḥ |
ko'sāvanātmā paramaḥ ka ātmā
tayorvivekaḥ kathametaducyatām || 49 ||

śrīguruvāca ||

dhanyo'si kṛtakṛtyo'si pāvita te kulaṃ tvayā |
yadavidyābandhamuktyā brahmībhavitumicchasi || 50 ||

ṛṇamocanakartāraḥ pituḥ santi sutādayaḥ |
bandhamocanakartā tu svasmādanyo na kaścana || 51 ||

mastakanyastabhārāderduḥkhamanyairnivāryate |
kṣudhādikṛtaduḥkhaṃ tu vinā svena na kenacit || 52 ||

44 There is a certain great means which puts an end to the fear of samsara. Crossing the sea of change by means of it, you will achieve the ultimate joy.

45 Supreme understanding springs from meditating on the meaning of Vedanta, and that is followed immediately by the elimination of the pain of samsara.

46 The practice of faith, devotion and meditation are declared by scripture to be the means to liberation for a seeker after liberation. He who perseveres in these will achieve freedom from the bondage to the body, created by ignorance.

47 Linked with ignorance, your supreme self has become involved in the bonds of non-self, and from that in samsara. The fire of the knowledge born from discriminating between these two will burn out the consequences of ignorance along with its very root.

The disciple asked:

48 Out of compassion hear this question I put to you, so that when I have heard the reply from your lips I will be able to put it into practice.

49 What exactly is bondage? How does it come about and remain? How is one freed from it? What exactly is non self? What is the Supreme Self? And how does one discriminate between them? Explain this to me.

The guru replied:

50 You are indeed blessed, for you have achieved the true purpose of life and sanctified your family, in that you seek deification by liberation from the bonds of ignorance.

51 Sons and suchlike are able to free their fathers from debts, but no-one can free someone else from bondage.

52 The pain of something like a weight on the head can be removed by others, but the pain of things like hunger can be put an end to by no-one but oneself.

pathyamauṣadhasevā ca kriyate yena rogiṇā |
ārogyasiddhirdṛṣṭāsya nānyānuṣṭhitakarmaṇā || 53 ||

vastusvarūpaṃ sphuṭabodhacakṣuṣā
svenaiva vedyaṃ na tu paṇḍitena |
candrasvarūpaṃ nijacakṣuṣaiva
jñātavyamanyairavagamyate kim || 54 ||

avidyākāmakarmādipāśabandhaṃ vimocitum |
kaḥ śaknuyādvinātmānaṃ kalpakoṭiśatairapi || 55 ||

na yogena na sāṃkhyena karmaṇā no na vidyayā |
brahmātmaikatvabodhena mokṣaḥ sidhyati nānyathā || 56 ||

vīṇāyā rūpasaundaryaṃ tantrīvādanasauṣṭhavam |
prajārañjjanamātraṃ tanna sāmrājyāya kalpate || 57 ||

vāgvaikharī śabdajharī śāstravyākhyānakauśalam |
vaiduṣyaṃ viduṣāṃ tadvadbhuktaye na tu muktaye || 58 ||

avijñāte pare tattve śāstrādhītistu niṣphalā |
vijñāte'pi pare tattve śāstrādhītistu niṣphalā || 59 ||

śabdajālaṃ mahāraṇyaṃ cittabhramaṇakāraṇam |
ataḥ prayatnājjñātavyaṃ tattvajñaistattvamātmanaḥ || 60 ||

ajñānasarpadaṣṭasya brahmajñānauṣadhaṃ vinā |
kimu vedaiśca śāstraiśca kimu mantraiḥ kimauṣadhaiḥ || 61 ||

na gacchati vinā pānaṃ vyādhirauṣadhaśabdataḥ |
vināparokṣānubhavaṃ brahmaśabdairna mucyate || 62 ||

53 A sick man is seen to get better by taking the appropriate medicine—not through treatment undertaken by others.

54 Reality can be experienced only with the eye of understanding, not just by a scholar. What the moon is like must be seen with one's own eyes. How can others do it for you?

55 Who but yourself can free you from the bonds of the fetters of things like ignorance, lust and the consequences of your actions—even in hundreds of thousands of years?

56 Liberation is achieved not by observances or by analysis, nor by deeds or learning, but only by the realization of one's oneness with God, and by no other means.

57 The beauty of a lute and skill in playing its cords can bring some pleasure to people but can hardly make you a king.

58 In the same way, speech alone, even a deluge of words, with scholarship and skill in commenting on the scriptures, may achieve some personal satisfaction but not liberation.

59 When the supreme reality is not understood, the study of the scriptures is useless, and study of the scriptures is useless when the supreme reality has been understood.

60 The tangle of words is a great forest which leads the mind off wandering about, so wise men should strive to get to know the truth about their own nature.

61 Except for the medicine of the knowledge of God, what use are Vedas, scriptures, mantras and such medicines when you have been bitten by the snake of ignorance?

62 An illness is not cured just by pronouncing the name of the medicine without drinking it, and you will not be liberated by just pronouncing the word God without direct experience.

akṛtvā dṛśyavilayamajñātvā tattvamātmanaḥ |
brahmaśabdaiḥ kuto muktiruktimātraphalairnṛṇām || 63 ||

akṛtvā śatrusaṃhāramagatvākhilabhūśriyam |
rājāhamiti śabdānno rājā bhavitumarhati || 64 ||

āptoktiṃ khananaṃ tathopariśilādyutkarṣaṇaṃ svīkṛtiṃ
nikṣepaḥ samapekṣate nahi bahiḥ śabdaistu nirgacchati |
tadvadbrahmavidopadeśamananadhyānādibhirlabhyate
māyākāryatirohitaṃ svamamalaṃ tattvaṃ na duryuktibhiḥ || 65 ||

tasmātsarvaprayatnena bhavabandhavimuktaye |
svaireva yatnaḥ kartavyo rogādāviva paṇḍitaiḥ || 66 ||

yastvayādya kṛtaḥ praśno varīyāñjchāstravinmataḥ |
sūtraprāyo nigūḍhārtho jñātavyaśca mumukṣubhiḥ || 67 ||

śṛṇuṣvāvahito vidvanyanmayā samudīryate |
tadetacchravaṇātsadyo bhavabandhādvimokṣyase || 68 ||

mokṣasya hetuḥ prathamo nigadyate
vairāgyamatyantamanityavastuṣu |
tataḥ śamaścāpi damastitikṣā
nyāsaḥ prasaktākhilakarmaṇāṃ bhṛśam || 69 ||

tataḥ śrutistanmananaṃ satattva
dhyānaṃ ciraṃ nityanirantaraṃ muneḥ |
tato'vikalpaṃ parametya vidvān
ihaiva nirvāṇasukhaṃ samṛcchati || 70 ||

yadboddhavyaṃ tavedānīmātmānātmavivecanam |
taducyate mayā samyakśrutvātmanyavadhāraya || 71 ||

63 How can one reach liberation by just pronouncing the word God without achieving the elimination of the visible universe and realizing the truth about one's own nature? It will just be a waste of speech.

64 One cannot become a king just by saying, "I am the king," without defeating one's enemies and taking possession of the country.

65 A buried treasure will not come out just by calling it, but needs a good map, digging, removal of obstructing stones and so on to get at it. In the same way the pure reality, hidden by the effects of Māyā, cannot be achieved by just abusing it, but by instruction from a knower of God, reflection, meditation and so on.

66 So the wise should strive with all their ability for liberation from the bonds of change, as they would in the case of sickness and things like that.

67 The question you have asked today is a good one in the opinion of those learned in the scriptures, to the point and full of meaning. It needs to be understood by those seeking liberation.

68 Listen carefully to what I say, master. By hearing this you will be freed from the bonds of change.

69 The primary basis of liberation is held to be total dispassion for everything impermanent, and after that peacefulness, restraint, patience, and the complete renunciation of scriptural observances.

70 After that the practicant finds there comes listening, reflection on what one has heard, and long meditation on the truth. Then the wise man will experience the supreme non-dual state and come here and now to the bliss of Nirvana.

71 When you have heard me fully explain what you need to know about the discrimination between self and non-self, then bear it in mind.

majjāsthimedaḥpalaraktacarma
tvagāhvayairdhātubhirebhiranvitam |
pādoruvakṣobhujapṛṣṭhamastakaiḥ
aṅgairupāṅgairupayuktametat || 72 ||
ahammametiprathitaṃ śarīraṃ
mohāspadaṃ sthūlamitīryate budhaiḥ |
nabhonabhasvaddahanāmbubhūmayaḥ
sūkṣmāṇi bhūtāni bhavanti tāni || 73 ||

parasparāṃśairmilitāni bhūtvā
sthūlāni ca sthūlaśarīrahetavaḥ |
mātrāstadīyā viṣayā bhavanti
śabdādayaḥ pañca sukhāya bhoktuḥ || 74 ||

ya eṣu mūḍhā viṣayeṣu baddhā
rāgorupāśena sudurdamena |
āyānti niryāntyadha ūrdhvamuccaiḥ
svakarmadūtena javena nītāḥ || 75 ||

śabdādibhiḥ pañcabhireva pañca
pañcatvamāpuḥ svaguṇena baddhāḥ |
kuraṅgamātaṅgapataṅgamīna
bhṛṅgā naraḥ pañcabhirañcitaḥ kim || 76 ||

doṣeṇa tīvro viṣayaḥ kṛṣṇasarpaviṣādapi |
viṣaṃ nihanti bhoktāraṃ draṣṭāraṃ cakṣuṣāpyayam || 77 ||

viṣayāśāmahāpāśādyo vimuktaḥ sudustyajāt |
sa eva kalpate muktyai nānyaḥ ṣaṭśāstravedyapi || 78 ||

āpātavairāgyavato mumukṣūn
bhavābdhipāraṃ pratiyātumudyatān |
āśāgraho majjayate'ntarāle
nigṛhya kaṇṭhe vinivartya vegāt || 79 ||

viṣayākhyagraho yena suviraktyasinā hataḥ |
sa gacchati bhavāmbhodheḥ pāraṃ pratyūhavarjitaḥ || 80 ||

72–73 The body, constituted of marrow, bone, fat, flesh, ligament and skin, and composed of feet, legs, chest, arms, back and head, is the seat of the "I" and "mine" delusion, and is known as the physical body by the wise, while space, air, fire, water and earth are the subtle elements.

74 When these various elements are combined, they form the physical body, while in themselves they constitute the objects of the senses, the five types of sound and so on, for the enjoyment of the individual.

75 The ignorant who are bound to the senses by the strong, hardly breakable bonds of desire, are borne here and there, up and down, in the control of their own karmic impulses.

76 Deer, elephant, moth, fish and wasp, these five have all died from attachment by their own volition to one of the five senses, sound etc., so what about the man who is attached to all five!

77 The effect of the senses is more deadly than even that of a cobra. Their poison kills a man who only just looks at them with his eyes.

78 Only he who is free from the terrible hankering after the senses which is so hard to overcome is fit for liberation, and no-one else, not even if he is an expert in the six branches of scripture.

79 The shark of longing grasps those whose desire for liberation is only superficial by the throat as they try to cross the sea of samsara and drowns them halfway.

80 He who has killed the shark of the senses with the sword of firm dispassion can cross the sea of samsara without impediment.

viṣamaviṣayamārgairgacchato'nacchabuddheḥ
pratipadamabhiyāto mṛtyurapyeṣa viddhi |
hitasujanaguruktyā gacchataḥ svasya yuktyā
prabhavati phalasiddhiḥ satyamityeva viddhi || 81 ||

mokṣasya kāṃkṣā yadi vai tavāsti
tyajātidūrādviṣayānviṣaṃ yathā |
pīyūṣavattoṣadayākṣamārjava
praśāntidāntīrbhaja nityamādarāt || 82 ||

anukṣaṇaṃ yatparihṛtya kṛtyaṃ
anādyavidyākṛtabandhamokṣaṇam |
dehaḥ parārtho'yamamuṣya poṣaṇe
yaḥ sajjate sa svamanena hanti || 83 ||

śarīrapoṣaṇārthī san ya ātmānaṃ didṛkṣati |
grāhaṃ dārudhiyā dhṛtvā nadi tartuṃ sa gacchati || 84 ||

moha eva mahāmṛtyurmumukṣorvapurādiṣu |
moho vinirjito yena sa muktipadamarhati || 85 ||

mohaṃ jahi mahāmṛtyuṃ dehadārasutādiṣu |
yaṃ jitvā munayo yānti tadviṣṇoḥ paramaṃ padam || 86 ||

tvaṅmāṃsarudhirasnāyumedomajjāsthisaṃkulam |
pūrṇaṃ mūtrapurīṣābhyāṃ sthūlaṃ nindyamidaṃ vapuḥ || 87 ||

pañcīkṛtebhyo bhūtebhyaḥ sthūlebhyaḥ pūrvakarmaṇā |
samutpannamidaṃ sthūlaṃ bhogāyatanamātmanaḥ
avasthā jāgarastasya sthūlārthānubhavo yataḥ || 88 ||

bāhyendriyaiḥ sthūlapadārthasevāṃ
srakcandanastryādivicitrarūpām |
karoti jīvaḥ svayametadātmanā
tasmātpraśastirvapuṣo'sya jāgare || 89 ||

81 Realize that death quickly waylays the senseless man who follows the uneven way of the senses, but that man achieves his purpose who follows the guidance of a true, compassionate guru. Know this as the truth.

82 If you really have a desire for liberation, avoid the senses from a great distance, as you would poison, and continually practice the nectar-like qualities of contentment, compassion, forbearance, honesty, calm and restraint.

83 He who neglects that which should be undertaken at all times, the liberation from the bonds created by beginningless ignorance, and gets stuck in pandering to the alien good of this body, is committing suicide by doing so.

84 He who seeks to know himself while pampering the body is crossing a river holding onto a crocodile in mistake for a log.

85 This infatuation with the body and such things is a great death for the seeker after liberation. He who has overcome this infatuation is worthy of liberation.

86 Overcome this great death of infatuation with such things as the body, wives and children. Sages who have overcome it go to the supreme realm of God.

87 This body is material and offensive, consisting of skin, flesh, blood, sinews, veins, fat, marrow and bones, and full of urine and excrement.

88 This material body, which arises from past action out of material elements formed by the combination of subtle elements, is the vehicle of sensation for the individual. This is the state of a waking person perceiving material objects.

89 The life force creates for itself, out of itself, material object of enjoyment by means of the external senses—such colourful things as flowers, perfumes, women, etc. That is why this has its fullest enjoyment in the waking state.

sarvāpi bāhyasaṃsāraḥ puruṣasya yadāśrayaḥ |
viddhi dehamidaṃ sthūlaṃ gṛhavadgṛhamedhinaḥ || 90 ||

sthūlasya saṃbhavajarāmaraṇāni dharmāḥ
sthaulyādayo bahuvidhāḥ śiśutādyavasthāḥ |
varṇāśramādiniyamā bahudhāmayāḥ syuḥ
pūjāvamānabahumānamukhā viśeṣāḥ || 91 ||

buddhīndriyāṇi śravaṇaṃ tvagakṣi
ghrāṇaṃ ca jivhā viṣayāvabodhanāt |
vākpāṇipādā gudamapyupasthaḥ
karmendriyāṇi pravaṇena karmasu || 92 ||

nigadyate'ntaḥkaraṇaṃ manodhīḥ
ahaṃkṛtiścittamiti svavṛttibhiḥ |
manastu saṃkalpavikalpanādibhiḥ
buddhiḥ padārthādhyavasāyadharmataḥ || 93 ||
atrābhimānādahamityahaṃkṛtiḥ |
svārthānusandhānaguṇena cittam || 94 ||

prāṇāpānavyānodānasamānā bhavatyasau prāṇaḥ |
svayameva vṛttibhedādvikṛtibhedātsuvarṇasalilādivat || 95 ||

vāgādi pañca śravaṇādi pañca
prāṇādi pañcābhramukhāni pañca |
buddhyādyavidyāpi ca kāmakarmaṇī
puryaṣṭakaṃ sūkṣmaśarīramāhuḥ || 96 ||

idaṃ śarīraṃ śṛṇu sūkṣmasaṃjñitaṃ
liṅgaṃ tvapañcīkṛtasaṃbhavam |
savāsanaṃ karmaphalānubhāvakaṃ
svājñānato'nādirupādhirātmanaḥ || 97 ||

90 See this material body, all that the external existence of a man depends on, as just like the house of a house-dweller.

91 Birth, old age and death are inherent in the physical body, as are such conditions as a heavy build and childhood, while there are different circumstances like caste and occupation, all sorts of diseases, and various different types of treatment, like respect and contempt to bear with.

92 Ears, skin, eyes, nose and tongue are organs of sense, since they enable the experience of objects, while voice, hands, feet and bowels are organs of action through their inclination to activity.

93–94 The inner sense is known variously as mind, understanding, the sense of agency, or volition, depending on its particular function—mind as imagining and analysing, understanding as establishing the truth of a matter, the sense of responsibility from relating everything to oneself, and volition as seeking its own good.

95 The one vital breath[2] takes the form of all the various breathings, exhalations and psychic currents and fields according to the various functions and characteristics, as do gold and water and such things.

96 The eight citadels of groups of five categories, starting respectively with speech, hearing, vital breath, ether, intelligence, ignorance desire and action, constitute what is known as the subtle body.

97 Hear that this higher body, also known as the subtle body, with its desires and its tendency to follow the course of causal conditioning, is derived from the undifferentiated elements, and is a beginningless superimposition, due to its ignorance, on the true self.

2 prāṇa.

svapno bhavatyasya vibhaktyavasthā
svamātraśeṣeṇa vibhāti yatra |
svapne tu buddhiḥ svayameva jāgrat
kālīnanānāvidhavāsanābhiḥ || 98 ||
kartrādibhāvaṃ pratipadya rājate
yatra svayaṃ bhāti hyayaṃ parātmā |
dhīmātrakopādhiraśeṣasākṣī
na lipyate tatkṛtakarmaleśaiḥ
yasmādasaṅgastata eva karmabhiḥ
na lipyate kiṃcidupādhinā kṛtaiḥ || 99 ||

sarvavyāpṛtikaraṇaṃ liṅgamidaṃ syāccidātmanaḥ puṃsaḥ |
vāsyādikamiva takṣṇastenaivātmā bhavatyasaṅgo'yam || 100 ||

andhatvamandatvapaṭutvadharmāḥ
sauguṇyavaiguṇyavaśāddhi cakṣuṣaḥ |
bādhiryamūkatvamukhāstathaiva
śrotrādidharmā na tu vetturātmanaḥ || 101 ||

ucchvāsaniḥśvāsavijṛmbhaṇakṣut
prasyandanādyutkramaṇādikāḥ kriyāḥ |
prāṇādikarmāṇi vadanti tajñāḥ
prāṇasya dharmāvaśanāpipāse || 102 ||

antaḥkaraṇameteṣu cakṣurādiṣu varṣmaṇi |
ahamityabhimānena tiṣṭhatyābhāsatejasā || 103 ||

ahaṃkāraḥ sa vijñeyaḥ kartā bhoktābhimānyayam |
sattvādiguṇayogena cāvasthātrayamaśnute || 104 ||

viṣayāṇāmānukūlye sukhī duḥkhī viparyaye |
sukhaṃ duḥkhaṃ ca taddharmaḥ sadānandasya nātmanaḥ || 105 ||

ātmārthatvena hi preyānviṣayo na svataḥ priyaḥ |
svata eva hi sarveṣāmātmā priyatamo yataḥ
tata ātmā sadānando nāsya duḥkhaṃ kadācana || 106 ||

98–99 Sleep is a distinct state of the self in which it shines by itself alone, whereas in dreaming the mind itself assumes the sense of agency due to the various desires of the waking state, while the supreme self shines on, on its own, as pure consciousness, the witness of everything from anger and such things on, without being itself affected by any of the actions performed by the mind. Since it is unattached to action, it is not affected by anything done by its superimpositions.

100 The subtle body is the vehicle of all operations for the self, like an axe and so on for the carpenter. The self itself is pure consciousness, and, as such, remains unattached.

101 Blindness, short-sightedness and sharp eyesight are simply due to the healthiness or defectiveness of the eye, just as such states as deafness and dumbness are conditions of the ear etc., not of the self, the knower.

102 Breathing in and out, yawning, sneezing and bodily secretions are described by experts as functions depending on the Inner Energy, while hunger and thirst for truth are functions of the Inner Energy direct.

103 The mind, as a reflection of Light, resides in the body with its senses, the eyes etc., through identifying itself with them.

104 The sense of responsibility is what feels itself as the doer and bearer of the consequences, and together with the three Attributes, purity etc., undergoes the three states.[3]

105 When the senses are favourable it is happy, and when they are not it is unhappy. So happiness and suffering are its attributes, and not those of the ever blissful self.

106 The senses are enjoyable only for the sake of oneself, not for themselves. The self is the most dear of everything, and consequently the self is ever blissful, and never experiences suffering.

3 of sleeping, dreaming, and waking.

yatsuṣuptau nirviṣaya ātmānando'nubhūyate |
śrutiḥ pratyakṣamaitihyamanumānaṃ ca jāgrati || 107 ||

avyaktanāmnī parameśaśaktiḥ
anādyavidyā triguṇātmikā parā |
kāryānumeyā sudhiyaiva māyā
yayā jagatsarvamidaṃ prasūyate || 108 ||

sannāpyasannāpyubhayātmikā no
bhinnāpyabhinnāpyubhayātmikā no |
sāṅgāpyanaṅgā hyubhayātmikā no
mahādbhutānirvacanīyarūpā || 109 ||

śuddhādvayabrahmavibhodhanāśyā
sarpabhramo rajjuvivekato yathā |
rajastamaḥsattvamiti prasiddhā
guṇāstadīyāḥ prathitaiḥ svakāryaiḥ || 110 ||

vikṣepaśaktī rajasaḥ kriyātmikā
yataḥ pravṛttiḥ prasṛtā purāṇī |
rāgādayo'syāḥ prabhavanti nityaṃ
duḥkhādayo ye manaso vikārāḥ || 111 ||

kāmaḥ krodho lobhadambhādyasūyā
ahaṃkārerṣyāmatsarādyāstu ghorāḥ |
dharmā ete rājasāḥ pumpravṛttiḥ
yasmādeṣā tadrajo bandhahetuḥ || 112 ||

eṣāvṛtirnāma tamoguṇasya
śaktirmayā vastvavabhāsate'nyathā |
saiṣā nidānaṃ puruṣasya saṃsṛteḥ
vikṣepaśakteḥ pravaṇasya hetuḥ || 113 ||

prajñāvānapi paṇḍito'pi caturo'pyatyantasūkṣmātmadṛg
vyālīḍhastamasā na vetti bahudhā saṃbodhito'pi sphuṭam |
bhrāntyāropitameva sādhu kalayatyālambate tadguṇān
hantāsau prabalā durantatamasaḥ śaktirmahatyāvṛtiḥ || 114 ||

107 That we experience the bliss of the self free from the senses in deep sleep is verified by the scriptures, by direct experience, by tradition and by deduction.

108 The so-called Inexpressible, the Lord's power, is the ultimate, beginningless ignorance made up of the three qualities,[4] the pure Māyā knowable through its effects, out of which this whole world is produced.

109 It cannot be said to either exist or not exist, to be divisible or indivisible, composite or unitary or both. It is amazing and indescribable.

110 It can be overcome by the realization of the pure non-dual God, like the false idea of a snake through the recognition of the rope. It is composed of the three qualities[2] of passion, dullness and purity, recognized by their effects.

111 The distracting power of passion is by nature active, and from it the primeval emanation of activity has taken place. The mental states like desire and pain continually arise from it as well.

112 Lust, anger, greed, pride, envy, self-importance and jealousy—these are the awful effects produced by passion. Consequently this passion quality is the cause of bondage.

113 The veiling effect of the dullness quality is the power that distorts the appearance of things. It is the cause of samsara in man, and what leads to the activation of the distracting power.[5]

114 Even a wise and learned man and an adept in the knowledge of the extremely subtle self can be overcome by dullness, and fail to realize it, even when demonstrated it in many different ways. What is presented by delusion he looks on as good, and grasps at its qualities. Such, alas, is the strength of the great veiling power of this awful dullness quality!

---

4 guṇas.
5 of passion.

abhāvanā vā viparītabhāvanā
asaṃbhāvanā vipratipattirasyāḥ |
saṃsargayuktaṃ na vimuñcati dhruvaṃ
vikṣepaśaktiḥ kṣapayatyajasram || 115 ||

ajñānamālasyajaḍatvanidrā
pramādamūḍhatvamukhāstamoguṇāḥ |
etaiḥ prayukto nahi vetti kiṃcin
nidrāluvatstambhavadeva tiṣṭhati || 116 ||

sattvaṃ viśuddhaṃ jalavattathāpi
tābhyāṃ militvā saraṇāya kalpate |
yatrātmabimbaḥ pratibimbitaḥ san
prakāśayatyarka ivākhilaṃ jaḍam || 117 ||

miśrasya sattvasya bhavanti dharmāḥ
tvamānitādyā niyamā yamādyāḥ |
śraddhā ca bhaktiśca mumukṣatā ca
daivī ca sampattirasannivṛttiḥ || 118 ||

viśuddhasattvasya guṇāḥ prasādaḥ
svātmānubhūtiḥ paramā praśāntiḥ |
tṛptiḥ praharṣaḥ paramātmaniṣṭhā
yayā sadānandarasaṃ samṛcchati || 119 ||

avyaktametattriguṇairniruktaṃ
tatkāraṇaṃ nāma śarīramātmanaḥ |
suṣuptiretasya vibhaktyavasthā
pralīnasarvendriyabuddhivṛttiḥ || 120 ||

sarvaprakārapramitipraśāntiḥ
bījātmanāvasthitireva buddheḥ |
suṣuptiretasya kila pratītiḥ
kiṃcinna vedmīti jagatprasiddheḥ || 121 ||

dehendriyaprāṇamano'hamādayaḥ
sarve vikārā viṣayāḥ sukhādayaḥ |
vyomādibhūtānyakhilaṃ na viśvaṃ
avyaktaparyantamidaṃ hyanātmā || 122 ||

115 Lack of sense or distorted understanding, lack of judgement, and bewilderment—these never leave him who is caught in this delusion, and the distracting power torments him continually.

116 Ignorance, laziness, drowsiness, sleep, carelessness, stupidity and so on are the effects of the dullness quality. One stuck in these does not understand anything, but remains as if asleep, like a wooden post.

117 Clear purity is like water, but combined with these other qualities it leads to samsara, though in this purity the nature of the self is reflected, like the disk of the sun illuminating the whole world.

118 In purity mixed with the other qualities virtues such as humility, restraint, truthfulness, faith, devotion, desire for liberation, spiritual tendencies and freedom from entanglement occur.

119 In real purity however the qualities which occur are contentment, self-understanding, supreme peace, fulfilment, joy and abiding in one's supreme self, through which one experiences real bliss.

120 This Inexpressible, described as made up of the three qualities,[6] is the active body of the self. Deep sleep is a special condition of it, in which the activity of all functions of awareness cease.

121 Deep sleep is the cessation of all forms of awareness, and the reversion of consciousness to a latent form of the self. "I knew nothing" is the universal experience.

122 The body, its functions, vital energies, the thinking mind, etc., and all forms, objects, enjoyment, etc. the physical elements such as the ether, in fact everything up to this Inexpressible are not one's true nature.

6 guṇas.

māyā māyākāryaṃ sarvaṃ mahadādidehaparyantam |
asadidamanātmatattvaṃ viddhi tvaṃ marumarīcikākalpam || 123 ||

atha te saṃpravakṣyāmi svarūpaṃ paramātmanaḥ |
yadvijñāya naro bandhānmuktaḥ kaivalyamaśnute || 124 ||

asti kaścitsvayaṃ nityamahaṃpratyayalambanaḥ |
avasthātrayasākṣī saṃpañcakośavilakṣaṇaḥ || 125 ||

yo vijānāti sakalaṃ jāgratsvapnasuṣuptiṣu |
buddhitadvṛttisadbhāvamabhāvamahamityayam || 126 ||

yaḥ paśyati svayaṃ sarvaṃ yaṃ na paśyati kaścana |
yaścetayati buddhyādi na tadyaṃ cetayatyayam || 127 ||

yena viśvamidaṃ vyāptaṃ yaṃ na vyāpnoti kiṃcana |
abhārūpamidaṃ sarvaṃ yaṃ bhāntyamanubhātyayam || 128 ||

yasya sannidhimātreṇa dehendriyamanodhiyaḥ |
viṣayeṣu svakīyeṣu vartante preritā iva || 129 ||

ahaṅkārādidehāntā viṣayāśca sukhādayaḥ |
vedyante ghaṭavadyena nityabodhasvarūpiṇā || 130 ||

eṣo'ntarātmā puruṣaḥ purāṇo
nirantarākhaṇḍasukhānubhūtiḥ |
sadaikarūpaḥ pratibodhamātro
yeneṣitā vāgasavaścaranti || 131 ||

atraiva sattvātmani dhīguhāyāṃ
avyākṛtākāśa uśatprakāśaḥ |
ākāśa uccai ravivatprakāśate
svatejasā viśvamidaṃ prakāśayan || 132 ||

123 Everything is the creation of Māyā from space itself down to the individual body. Look on it all as a desert mirage, unreal and not yourself.

124 Now I will instruct you in the true nature of your supreme self, by understanding which a man is freed from his bonds and achieves final fulfilment.

125 There *is* something your own, unchanging, the "I", the substratum, the basis, which is the triple observer, distinct from the five sheaths.

126 The awareness that knows everything whether waking, dreaming or in deed sleep, and whether or not there is movement in the mind, that is the "I".

127 It is that which experiences everything, but which nothing else can experience, which thinks through the intelligence etc., but which nothing else can think. -

128 It is that by which all this is filled, but which nothing else can fill, and which, in shining, makes all this shines as well.

129 It is that whose mere presence makes the body, bodily senses, and mind etc. keep to their appropriate functions like servants.

130 It is that by which everything from the ego function down to the body is known like an earthen vessel, for its very nature is everlasting consciousness.

131 This is one's inmost nature, the eternal Person, whose very essence is unbroken awareness of happiness, who is ever unchanging and pure consciousness, and in obedience to whom the various bodily function continue.

132 In one of pure nature, the morning light of the Unmanifest shines even here in the cave of the mind, illuminating all this with its glory, like the sun up there in space.

jñātā mano'haṃkṛtivikriyāṇāṃ
dehendriyaprāṇakṛtakriyāṇām |
ayo'gnivattānanuvartamāno
na ceṣṭate no vikaroti kiṃcana || 133 ||

na jāyate no mriyate na vardhate
na kṣīyate no vikaroti nityaḥ |
vilīyamāne'pi vapuṣyamuṣmin
na līyate kumbha ivāmbaraṃ svayam || 134 ||

prakṛtivikṛtibhinnaḥ śuddhabodhasvabhāvaḥ
sadasadidamaśeṣaṃ bhāsayannirviśeṣaḥ |
vilasati paramātmā jāgradādiṣvavasthā
svahamahamiti sākṣātsākṣirūpeṇa buddheḥ || 135 ||

niyamitamanasāmuṃ tvaṃ svamātmānamātmany
ayamahamiti sākṣādviddhi buddhiprasādāt |
janimaraṇataraṅgāpārasaṃsārasindhuṃ
pratara bhava kṛtārtho brahmarūpeṇa saṃsthaḥ || 136 ||

atrānātmanyahamiti matirbandha eṣo'sya puṃsaḥ
prāpto'jñānājjananamaraṇakleśasaṃpātahetuḥ |
yenaivāyaṃ vapuridamasatsatyamityātmabuddhyā
puṣyatyukṣatyavati viṣayaistantubhiḥ kośakṛdvat || 137 ||

atasmiṃstadbuddhiḥ prabhavati vimūḍhasya tamasā
vivekābhāvādvai sphurati bhujage rajjudhiṣaṇā |
tato'narthavrāto nipatati samādāturadhikaḥ
tato yo'sadgrāhaḥ sa hi bhavati bandhaḥ śṛṇu sakhe || 138 ||

akhaṇḍanityādvayabodhaśaktyā
sphurantamātmānamanantavaibhavam |
samāvṛṇotyāvṛtiśaktireṣā
tamomayī rāhurivārkabimbam || 139 ||

133 That which knows the thinking mind and ego functions takes its form from the body with its senses and other functions, like fire does in a ball of iron, but it neither acts nor changes in any way.

134 It is never born, never dies, grows, decays, or changes. Even when the body is destroyed it does not cease to be, like the space in an earthen vessel.

135 The true self, of the nature of pure consciousness, and separate from the productions of nature, illuminates all this, real and unreal, without itself changing. It plays in the states of waking and so on, as the foundation sense of 'I exist', as the awareness, witness of all experience.

136 By means of a trained mind, and thanks to your faculty of understanding, experience in practice the true self of this 'I exist' in yourself, cross the ocean of Samsara's waves of birth and death, and established in the nature of God, and achieve the goal.[7]

137 Seeing 'This is me' in what is not really oneself, this is man's bondage, the result of ignorance and the cause of the descent into the pain of birth and death. It is because of this that one sees this unreal body as real, and identifying oneself with it, feeds it and cares for it with the senses, like a grub in its cocoon.

138 One who is confused by lack of clarity sees something which is not there, like a man mistaking a rope for a snake through lack of understanding, and experiencing great pain etc. from mistakenly taking hold of it. So, my friend, hear this—Bondage is thinking that something non-existent exists.

139 This obscuring power conceals the infinite glory of one's true self which radiates with its indivisible, eternal and unified power of understanding, like an eclipse obscures the sun's disk, and creates darkness.

7 of life.

tirobhūte svātmanyamalataratejovati pumān
anātmānaṃ mohādahamiti śarīraṃ kalayati |
tataḥ kāmakrodhaprabhṛtibhiramuṃ bandhanaguṇaiḥ
paraṃ vikṣepākhyā rajasa uruśaktirvyathayati || 140 ||

mahāmohagrāhagrasanagalitātmāvagamano
dhiyo nānāvasthāṃ svayamabhinayaṃstadguṇatayā |
apāre saṃsare viṣayaviṣapūre jalanidhau
nimajyonmajyāyaṃ bhramati kumatiḥ kutsitagatiḥ || 141 ||

bhānuprabhāsaṃjanitābhrapaṅktiḥ
bhānuṃ tirodhāya vijṛmbhate yathā |
ātmoditāhaṃkṛtirātmatattvaṃ
tathā tirodhāya vijṛmbhate svayam || 142 ||

kavalitadinanārthe durdine sāndrameghaiḥ
vyathayati himajhaṃjhāvāyurugro yathaitān |
aviratatamasātmanyāvṛte mūḍhabuddhiṃ
kṣapayati bahuduḥkhaistīvravikṣepaśaktiḥ || 143 ||

etābhyāmeva śaktibhyāṃ bandhaḥ puṃsaḥ samāgataḥ |
yābhyāṃ vimohito dehaṃ matvātmānaṃ bhramatyayam || 144 ||

bījaṃ saṃsṛtibhūmijasya tu tamo dehātmadhīraṅkuro
rāgaḥ pallavamambu karma tu vapuḥ skandhoo'savaḥ śākhikāḥ |
agrāṇīndriyasaṃhatiśca viṣayāḥ puṣpāṇi duḥkhaṃ phalaṃ
nānākarmasamudbhavaṃ bahuvidhaṃ bhoktātra jīvaḥ khagaḥ || 145 ||

ajñānamūlo'yamanātmabandho
naisargiko'nādirananta īritaḥ |
janmāpyayavyādhijarādiduḥkha
pravāhapātaṃ janayatyamuṣya || 146 ||

nāstrairna śastrairanilena vanhinā
chettuṃ na śakyo na ca karmakoṭibhiḥ |
vivekavijñānamahāsinā vinā
dhātuḥ prasādena śitena mañjunā || 147 ||

140 When he has lost sight of his true self, immaculate and resplendent, a man identifies himself with his body out of ignorance. Then the great so-called dispersive power torments him with its fetters of continuous desire, hatred etc.

141 When a man has fallen to the state of being swallowed up by the great shark of ignorance, he assumes to himself the various states superimposed upon him, and in a pitiful state wanders rising and sinking in the great ocean of Samsara.

142 Just as cloud formations, arising from the suns rays, obscure the sun and fill the sky, so the sense of self-identity, arising from one's true nature, obscures the existence of the true self and itself fills experience.

143 Just as the thick clouds covering the sun on a bad day are buffeted by cold, howling blasts of wind, so, when one's true nature is obscured by deep ignorance, the strong dispersive power torments the confused understanding with many afflictions.

144 It is from these powers that man's bondage has arisen. Confused by them, he mistakes the body for himself and wanders in error.

145 The seed of the Samsara tree is ignorance, identification with the body is its shoot, desire is its first leaves, activity its water, the bodily frame its trunk, the vital forces its branches, the faculties its twigs, the senses its flowers, the manifold pains arising from various actions its fruit, and the bird on it is the individual experiencing them.

146 Ignorance is the root of this bondage to what is not one's true nature, a bondage which is called beginningless and endless. It gives rise to the long course of suffering—birth, death, sickness, old age, etc.

147 It cannot be destroyed by weapons, wind or fire, nor even by countless actions—by nothing, in fact, except by the wonderful sword of wisdom, sharpened by God's grace.

śrutipramāṇaikamateḥ svadharma
niṣṭhā tayaivātmaviśuddhirasya |
viśuddhabuddheḥ paramātmavedanaṃ
tenaiva saṃsārasamūlanāśaḥ || 148 ||

kośairannamayādyaiḥ pañcabhirātmā na saṃvṛto bhāti |
nijaśaktisamutpannaiḥ śaivālapaṭalairivāmbu vāpīstham || 149 ||

tacchaivālāpanaye samyaksalilaṃ pratīyate śuddham |
tṛṣṇāsantāpaharaṃ sadyaḥ saukhyapradaṃ paraṃ puṃsaḥ || 150 ||

pañcānāmapi kośānāmapavāde vibhātyayaṃ śuddhaḥ |
nityānandaikarasaḥ pratyagrūpaḥ paraḥ svayaṃjyotiḥ || 151 ||

ātmānātmavivekaḥ kartavyo bandhamuktaye viduṣā |
tenaivānandī bhavati svaṃ vijñāya saccidānandam || 152 ||

muñjādiṣīkāmiva dṛśyavargāt
pratyañcamātmānamasaṅgamakriyam |
vivicya tatra pravilāpya sarvaṃ
tadātmanā tiṣṭhati yaḥ sa muktaḥ || 153 ||

deho'yamannabhavano'nnamāyāstu kośaḥ
cānnena jīvati vinaśyati tadvihīnaḥ |
tvakcarmamāṃsarudhirāsthipurīṣarāśiḥ
nāyaṃ svayaṃ bhavitumarhati nityaśuddhaḥ || 154 ||

pūrvaṃ janeradhimṛterapi nāyamasti
jātakṣaṇaḥ kṣaṇaguṇo'niyatasvabhāvaḥ |
naiko jaḍaśca ghaṭavatparidṛśyamānaḥ
svātmā kathaṃ bhavati bhāvavikāravettā || 155 ||

pāṇipādādimāndeho nātmā vyaṅge'pi jīvanāt |
tattacchakteranāśācca na niyamyo niyāmakaḥ || 156 ||

148 He who is devoted to the authority of the scriptures achieves steadiness in his religious life, and that brings inner purity. The man of pure understanding comes to the experience of his true nature, and by this Samsara is destroyed, root and all.

149 One's true nature does not shine out when covered by the five sheaths, material and otherwise, although they are the product of its own power, like the water in a pool, covered with algae.

150 On removing the algae, the clean, thirst-quenching and joy-inducing water is revealed to a man.

151 When the five sheaths have been removed, the supreme light shines forth, pure, eternally blissful, single in essence, and within.

152 To be free from bondage the wise man must practise discrimination between self and non-self. By that alone he will become full of joy, recognizing himself as Being, Consciousness and Bliss.

153 Just as one separates a blade of grass from its sheaths, so by discriminating one's true nature as internal, unattached and free from action, and abandoning all else, one is free and identified only with one's true self.

154 This body is the product of food, and constitutes the material sheath. It depends on food and dies without it. It is a mass of skin, flesh, blood, bones and uncleanness. It is not fit to see as oneself, who is ever pure.

155 The body did not exist before birth, nor will it exist after death. It is born for a moment, its qualities are momentary, and it is inherently changing. It is not a single thing, but inert, and should be viewed like an earthen pot. How could it be one's true self, which is the observer of changing phenomena?

156 Made up of arms and legs and so on, the body cannot be one's true self as it can live on without various limbs, and other faculties persist without them. What is controlled cannot be the controller.

dehataddharmatatkarmatadavasthādisākṣiṇaḥ |
sata eva svataḥsiddhaṃ tadvailakṣaṇyamātmanaḥ || 157 ||

śalyarāśirmāṃsalipto malapūrṇo'tikaśmalaḥ |
kathaṃ bhavedayaṃ vettā svayametadvilakṣaṇaḥ || 158 ||

tvaṅmāṃsamedo'sthipurīṣarāśā
vahaṃmatiṃ mūḍhajanaḥ karoti |
vilakṣaṇaṃ vetti vicāraśīlo
nijasvarūpaṃ paramārtha bhūtam || 159 ||

deho'hamityeva jaḍasya buddhiḥ
dehe ca jīve viduṣastvahaṃdhīḥ |
vivekavijñānavato mahātmano
brahmāhamityeva matiḥ sadātmani || 160 ||

atrātmabuddhiṃ tyaja mūḍhabuddhe
tvaṅmāṃsamedo'sthipurīṣarāśau |
sarvātmani brahmaṇi nirvikalpe
kuruṣva śānti paramāṃ bhajasva || 161 ||

dehendriyādāvasati bhramoditāṃ
vidvānahaṃ tāṃ na jahāti yāvat |
tāvanna tasyāsti vimuktivārtāpy
astveṣa vedāntanayāntadarśī || 162 ||

chāyāśarīre pratibimbagātre
yatsvapnadehe hṛdi kalpitāṅge |
yathātmabuddhistava nāsti kācij
jīvaccharīre ca tathaiva māstu || 163 ||

dehātmadhīreva nṛṇāmasaddhiyāṃ
janmādiduḥkhaprabhavasya bījam |
yatastatastvaṃ jahi tāṃ prayatnāt
tyakte tu citte na punarbhavāśā || 164 ||

karmendriyaiḥ pañcabhirañcito'yaṃ
prāṇo bhavetprāṇamāyāstu kośaḥ |
yenātmavānannamayo'nupūrṇaḥ
pravartate'sau sakalakriyāsu || 165 ||

157 While the body of the observer is of a specific nature, behaviour and situation, it is clear that the nature of one's true self is devoid of characteristics.

158 How could the body, which is a heap of bones, covered with flesh, full of filth and highly impure, be oneself, the featureless observer?

159 The deluded man makes the assumption that he is the mass of skin, flesh, fat bones and filth, while the man who is strong in discrimination knows himself as devoid of characteristics, the innate supreme Reality.

160 "I am the body" is the opinion of the fool. "I am body and soul" is the view of the scholar, while for the great-souled, discriminating man, his inner knowledge is "I am God".

161 Get rid of the opinion of yourself as this mass of skin, flesh, fat, bones and filth, foolish one, and make yourself instead the self of everything, the God beyond all thought, and enjoy supreme peace.

162 While the scholar does not overcome his sense of 'I am this' in the body and its faculties, there is no liberation for him, however much he may be learned in religion and philosophy.

163 Just as you have no self identification with your shadow-body, reflection-body, dream-body or imagination-body, so you should not have with the living body either.

164 Identification of oneself with the body is the seed of the pain of birth etc. in people attached to the unreal, so get rid of it with care. When this thought is eliminated, there is no more desire for rebirth.

165 The vital energy joined to the five activities forms the vitality sheath, by which the material sheath is filled, and engages in all these activities.

naivātmāpi prāṇamayo vāyuvikāro
gantāgantā vāyuvadantarbahireṣaḥ |
yasmātkiṃcitkvāpi na vettīṣṭamaniṣṭaṃ
svaṃ vānyaṃ vā kiṃcana nityaṃ paratantraḥ || 166 ||

jñānendriyāṇi ca manaśca manomāyāḥ syāt
kośo mamāhamiti vastuvikalpahetuḥ |
saṃjñādibhedakalanākalito balīyāṃs
tatpūrvakośamabhipūrya vijṛmbhate yaḥ || 167 ||

pañcendriyaiḥ pañcabhireva hotṛbhiḥ
pracīyamāno viṣayājyadhārayā |
jājvalyamāno bahuvāsanendhanaiḥ
manomayāgnirdahati prapañcam || 168 ||

na hyastyavidyā manaso'tiriktā
mano hyavidyā bhavabandhahetuḥ |
tasminvinaṣṭe sakalaṃ vinaṣṭaṃ
vijṛmbhite'sminsakalaṃ vijṛmbhate || 169 ||

svapne'rthaśūnye sṛjati svaśaktyā
bhoktrādiviśvaṃ mana eva sarvam |
tathaiva jāgratyapi no viśeṣaḥ
tatsarvametanmanaso vijṛmbhaṇam || 170 ||

suṣuptikāle manasi pralīne
naivāsti kiṃcitsakalaprasiddheḥ |
ato manaḥkalpiteva puṃsaḥ
saṃsāra etasya na vastuto'sti || 171 ||

vāyunānīyate medhaḥ punastenaiva nīyate |
manasā kalpyate bandho mokṣastenaiva kalpyate || 172 ||

dehādisarvaviṣaye parikalpya rāgaṃ
badhnāti tena puruṣaṃ paśuvadguṇena |
vairasyamatra viṣavatsuvudhāya paścād
enaṃ vimocayati tanmana eva bandhāt || 173 ||

166 The Breath, being a product of the vital energy, is not one's true nature either. Like the air, it enters and leaves the body, and knows neither its own or other people's good or bad, dependent as it is on something else.

167 The faculty of knowledge and the mind itself constitute the mind-made sheath, the cause of such distinctions as 'me' and 'mine'. It is strong and has the faculty of creating distinctions of perception etc., and works itself through the vitality sheath.

168 The mind-made fire burns the multiplicity of experience in the fuel of numerous desires of the senses presented as oblations in the form of sense objects by the five senses like five priests.

169 There is no such thing as ignorance beyond the thinking mind. Thought is itself ignorance, the cause of the bondage of becoming. When thought is eliminated, everything else is eliminated. When thought increases everything else increases.

170 In sleep which is devoid of actual experience, it is the mind alone which produces everything, the experiencer and everything else, by its own power, and in the waking state there is no difference. All this is the product of the mind.

171 In deep sleep when the thinking mind has gone into abeyance there is nothing, by every one's experience, so man's Samsara is a mind creation, and has no real existence.

172 Cloud is gathered by the wind, and is driven away by it too. Bondage is imagined by the mind, and liberation is imagined by it too.

173 By dwelling with desire on the body and other senses the mind binds a man like an animal with a rope, and the same mind liberates him from the bond by creating simple distaste for the senses as if they were poison.

tasmānmanaḥ kāraṇamasya jantoḥ
bandhasya mokṣasya ca vā vidhāne |
bandhasya heturmalinaṃ rajoguṇaiḥ
mokṣasya śuddhaṃ virajastamaskam || 174 ||

vivekavairāgyaguṇātirekāc
chuddhatvamāsādya mano vimuktyai |
bhavatyato buddhimato mumukṣos
tābhyāṃ dṛḍhābhyāṃ bhavitavyamagre || 175 ||

mano nāma mahāvyāghro viṣayāraṇyabhūmiṣu |
caratyatra na gacchantu sādhavo ye mumukṣavaḥ || 176 ||

manaḥ prasūte viṣayānaśeṣān
sthūlātmanā sūkṣmatayā ca bhoktuḥ |
śarīravarṇāśramajātibhedān
guṇakriyāhetuphalāni nityam || 177 ||

asaṅgacidrūpamamuṃ vimohya
dehendriyaprāṇaguṇairnibaddhya |
ahaṃmameti bhramāyātyajasraṃ
manaḥ svakṛtyeṣu phalopabhuktiṣu || 178 ||

adhyāsadoṣātpuruṣasya saṃsṛtiḥ
adhyāsabandhastvamunaiva kalpitaḥ |
rajastamodoṣavato'vivekino
janmādiduḥkhasya nidānametat || 179 ||

ataḥ prāhurmano'vidyāṃ paṇḍitāstattvadarśinaḥ |
yenaiva bhrāmyate viśvaṃ vāyunevābhramaṇḍalam || 180 ||

tanmanaḥśodhanaṃ kāryaṃ prayatnena mumukṣuṇā |
viśuddhe sati caitasminmuktiḥ karaphalāyate || 181 ||

mokṣaikasaktyā viṣayeṣu rāgaṃ
nirmūlya saṃnyasya ca sarvakarma |
sacchraddhayā yaḥ śravaṇādiniṣṭho
rajaḥsvabhāvaṃ sa dhunoti buddheḥ || 182 ||

174 Thus the mind is the cause of a man's finding both bondage and liberation. When soiled with the attribute of desire it is the cause of bondage, and when clear of desire and ignorance it is the cause of liberation.

175 By achieving the purity of an habitual discrimination and dispassion, the mind is inclined to liberation, so the wise seeker after liberation should first develop these.

176 A great tiger known as the mind lives in the forest of the senses, so pious seekers after liberation should not go there.

177 The mind continually presents endless coarse or subtle sense experiences for a person—all the differences of physique, caste, state and birth, and the fruits resulting from attributes and actions.

178 The mind continually confuses that which is by nature unattached, binding it with the fetters of body, senses and faculties so that it thinks in terms of 'me' and 'mine' in the experiences he is achieving.

179 Man's Samsara is due to the error of additions,[8] and it is from the mind's imagination that the bondage of these additions comes. This is the cause of the pain of birth and so on for the man without discrimination who is filled with desire and ignorance.

180 That is why the wise who have experienced reality call the mind ignorance, for it is by that that everything is driven, like a mass of clouds by the wind.

181 So the mind must be earnestly purified by the seeker after liberation. Once it is purified, the fruit of liberation comes easily to hand.

182 Completely rooting out desire for the senses and abandoning all activity by one-pointed devotion to liberation, he who is established with true faith in study etc., purges away the passion from his understanding.

8 to his true nature.

manomayo nāpi bhavetparātmā
hyādyantavattvātpariṇāmibhāvāt |
duḥkhātmakatvādviṣayatvahetoḥ
draṣṭā hi dṛśyātmatayā na dṛṣṭaḥ || 183 ||

buddhirbuddhīndriyaiḥ sārdhaṃ savṛttiḥ kartṛlakṣaṇaḥ |
vijñānamāyākośaḥ syātpuṃsaḥ saṃsārakāraṇam || 184 ||

anuvrajaccitpratibimbaśaktiḥ
vijñānasaṃjñaḥ prakṛtervikāraḥ |
jñānakriyāvānahamityajasraṃ
dehendriyādiṣvabhimanyate bhṛśam || 185 ||

anādikālo'yamahaṃsvabhāvo
jīvaḥ samastavyavahāravoḍhā |
karoti karmāṇyapi pūrvavāsanaḥ
puṇyānyapuṇyāni ca tatphalāni || 186 ||
bhuṅkte vicitrāsvapi yoniṣu vrajan
nāyāti niryātyadha ūrdhvameṣaḥ |
asyaiva vijñānamāyāsya jāgrat
svapnādyavasthāḥ sukhaduḥkhabhogaḥ || 187 ||

dehādiniṣṭhāśramadharmakarma
guṇābhimānaḥ satataṃ mameti |
vijñānakośo'yamatiprakāśaḥ
prakṛṣṭasānnidhyavaśātparātmanaḥ |
ato bhavatyeṣa upādhirasya
yadātmadhīḥ saṃsarati bhrameṇa || 188 ||

yo'yaṃ vijñānamāyāḥ prāṇeṣu hṛdi sphuratyayaṃ jyotiḥ |
kūṭasthaḥ sannātmā kartā bhoktā bhavatyupādhisthaḥ || 189 ||

svayaṃ paricchedamupetya buddheḥ
tādātmyadoṣeṇa paraṃ mṛṣātmanaḥ |
sarvātmakaḥ sannapi vīkṣate svayaṃ
svataḥ pṛthaktvena mṛdo ghaṭāniva || 190 ||

183 What is mind-made cannot be one's true nature, because it is changeable, having a beginning and an end, because it is subject to pain, and because it is itself an object. The knower cannot be seen as an object of consciousness.

184 The intellect along with its faculties, its activities and its characteristic of seeing itself as the agent, constitutes the knowledge sheath which is the cause of man's samsara.

185 Intellectual knowledge which as a function is a distant reflection of pure consciousness, is a natural faculty. It continually creates the awareness 'I exist', and strongly identifies itself with the body, its faculties and so on.

186–87 This sense of self is from beginningless time. As the person it is the agent of all relative occupations. Through its proclivities from the past it performs good and bad actions, and bears their fruit.
After experiencing them it is born in all sorts of different wombs, and progresses up and down in life, the experiencer of the knowledge-created states of waking, sleeping etc., and of pleasure and pain.

188 It always sees as its own such things as the body, and its circumstances, states, duties, actions and functions. The knowledge sheath is very impressive owing to its inherent affinity to the supreme self, which, identifying itself with the superimposition, experiences samsara because of this illusion.

189 This knowledge-created light shines among the faculties of the heart, and the true self, although itself motionless, becomes the actor and the experiencer while identified with this superimposition.

190 Allied to the intellect, just a part of itself, although the true self of everything, and beyond the limitations of such an existence, it identifies itself with this illusory self—as if clay were to identify itself with earthen jars.

upādhisaṃbandhavaśātparātmā
hyupādhidharmānanubhāti tadguṇaḥ |
ayovikārānavikārivanhivat
sadaikarūpo'pi paraḥ svabhāvāt || 191 ||

śiṣya uvāca ||

bhrameṇāpyanyathā vāstu jīvabhāvaḥ parātmanaḥ |
tadupādheranāditvānnānādernāśa iṣyate || 192 ||

ato'sya jīvabhāvo'pi nityā bhavati saṃsṛtiḥ |
na nivarteta tanmokṣaḥ kathaṃ me śrīguro vada || 193 ||

śrīgururuvāca ||

samyakpṛṣṭaṃ tvayā vidvansāvadhānena tacchṛṇu |
prāmāṇikī na bhavati bhrāntyā mohitakalpanā || 194 ||

bhrāntiṃ vinā tvasaṅgasya niṣkriyasya nirākṛteḥ |
na ghaṭetārthasaṃbandho nabhaso nīlatādivat || 195 ||

svasya draṣṭurnirguṇasyākriyasya
pratyagbodhānandarūpasya buddheḥ |
bhrāntyā prāpto jīvabhāvo na satyo
mohāpāye nāstyavastusvabhāvāt || 196 ||

yāvadbhrāntistāvadevāsya sattā
mithyājñānojjṛmbhitasya pramādāt |
rajjvāṃ sarpo bhrāntikālīna eva
bhrānternāśe naiva sarpo'pi tadvat || 197 ||

anāditvamavidyāyāḥ kāryasyāpi tatheṣyate |
utpannāyāṃ tu vidyāyāmāvidyakamanādyapi || 198 ||
prabodhe svapnavatsarvaṃ sahamūlaṃ vinaśyati |
anādyapīdaṃ no nityaṃ prāgabhāva iva sphuṭam || 199 ||

191 In conjunction with such additional qualities, the supreme self seems to manifest the same characteristics, just as the undifferentiated fire seems to take on the qualities of the iron it heats.

The disciple said:

192 Whether it is by mistake or for some other reason that the supreme self has become a living being, the identification is beginningless, and there can be no end to what has no beginning.

193 So the state of a living being is going to be a continual samsara, and there can be no liberation for it. Can you explain this to me?

The teacher said:

194 You have asked the right question, wise one, so now listen. The mistaken imagination of illusion is not a reality.

195 Outside of illusion no attachment can come about for what is by nature unattached, actionless and formless, as in the case of blueness and space.[9]

196 Existence as a living being, due to the mistaken intellect identifying itself with its own light, the inner joy of understanding, beyond qualities and beyond activity does not really exist, so when the illusion ceases, it does too, having no real existence of its own.

197 So long as the illusion exists, it too has existence, created by the confusion of misunderstanding, in the same way that a rope seems to be a snake so long as the illusion persists. When the illusion comes to an end, so does the snake.

198–99 Ignorance and its effects are seen as beginningless until with the arising of insight, ignorance and its effects are destroyed along with its root, even if beginningless, like dreams on awaking from sleep. Even if beginningless this world of appearances is not eternal—like something originally non-existent.

9 the sky.

anāderapi vidhvaṃsaḥ prāgabhāvasya vīkṣitaḥ |
yadbuddhyupādhisaṃbandhātparikalpitamātmani || 200 ||
jīvatvaṃ na tato'nyastu svarūpeṇa vilakṣaṇaḥ |
saṃbandhastvātmano buddhyā mithyājñānapuraḥsaraḥ || 201 ||

vinivṛttirbhavettasya samyagjñānena nānyathā |
brahmātmaikatvavijñānaṃ samyagjñānaṃ śrutermatam || 202 ||

tadātmānātmanoḥ samyagvivekenaiva sidhyati |
tato vivekaḥ kartavyaḥ pratyagātmasadātmanoḥ || 203 ||

jalaṃ paṅkavadatyantaṃ paṅkāpāye jalaṃ sphuṭam |
yathā bhāti tathātmāpi doṣābhāve sphuṭaprabhaḥ || 204 ||

asannivṛttau tu sadātmanā sphuṭaṃ
pratītiretasya bhavetpratīcaḥ |
tato nirāsaḥ karaṇīya eva
sadātmanaḥ sādhvahamādivastunaḥ || 205 ||

ato nāyaṃ parātmā syādvijñānamayāśabdabhāk |
vikāritvājjaḍatvācca paricchinnatvahetutaḥ |
dṛśyatvādvyabhicāritvānnānityo nitya iṣyate || 206 ||

ānandapratibimbacumbitatanurvṛttistamojṛmbhitā
syādānandamāyāḥ priyādiguṇakaḥ sveṣṭārthalābhodayaḥ |
puṇyasyānubhave vibhāti kṛtināmānandarūpaḥ svayaṃ
sarvo nandati yatra sādhu tanubhṛnmātraḥ prayatnaṃ vinā || 207 ||

ānandamāyākośasya suṣuptau sphūrtirutkaṭā |
svapnajāgarayorīṣadiṣṭasaṃdarśanāvinā || 208 ||

200–01 Even if beginningless, something originally non-existent is seen to come to an end. In the same way the living organism which is thought to belong to oneself through its identification with the intellect, does not really exist. On the other hand, the true self is quite distinct from it, and the identification of oneself with the intellect is due to misunderstanding.

202 The cessation of that wrong identification is achieved by right understanding, and by no other means. Right understanding is held by scripture to be the recognition of the oneness of God and oneself.

203 This recognition is achieved by right discrimination between what is truly oneself and what is not, so one must develop this discrimination between the conventional self and one's true self.

204 Like very muddy water, which is clearly water again when the mud is removed, one's true self shines forth again when the contamination is removed.

205 When the non-existent is removed the individual is disclosed as the supreme self, so one must see to the removal of thoughts about "me" and suchlike from oneself.

206 The level of sense awareness cannot be one's true self since it is changeable, physical, restricted, a sense-object and intermittent. What is transient should not be mistaken what is eternal.

207 The level of pleasure is the aspect of ignorance which is a sort of reflection the blissfulness of the true self. Its attributes are the qualities of enjoyment and so on, which are experienced when an enjoyable object is present. It presents itself spontaneously to those fortunate enough to experience the fruits of good deeds, something from which everyone experiences great pleasure without trying to.

208 The pleasure level is manifest at its fullest extent in deep sleep, whereas in dreams and the waking state it is only partially manifest, stimulated by such things as the sight of enjoyable objects.

naivāyamānandamāyāḥ parātmā
sopādhikatvātprakṛtervikārāt |
kāryatvahetoḥ sukṛtakriyāyā
vikārasaṅghātasamāhitatvāt || 209 ||

pañcānāmapi kośānāṃ niṣedhe yuktitaḥ śruteḥ |
tanniṣedhāvadhi sākṣī bodharūpo'vaśiṣyate || 210 ||

yo'yamātmā svayaṃjyotiḥ pañcakośavilakṣaṇaḥ |
avasthātrayasākṣī sannirvikāro nirañjanaḥ
sadānandaḥ sa vijñeyaḥ svātmatvena vipaścitā || 211 ||

śiṣya uvāca ||

mithyātvena niṣiddheṣu kośeṣveteṣu pañcasu |
sarvābhāvaṃ vinā kiṃcinna paśyāmyatra he guro
vijñeyaṃ kimu vastvasti svātmanātmavipaścitā || 212 ||

śrīgururuvāca ||

satyamuktaṃ tvayā vidannipuṇo'si vicāraṇe |
ahamādivikārāste tadabhāvo'yamapyanu || 213 ||
sarve yenānubhūyante yaḥ svayaṃ nānubhūyate |
tamātmānaṃ veditāraṃ viddi buddhyā susūkṣmayā || 214 ||

tatsākṣikaṃ bhavettattadyadyadyenānubhūyate |
kasyāpyananubhūtārthe sākṣitvaṃ nopayujyate || 215 ||

asau svasākṣiko bhāvo yataḥ svenānubhūyate |
ataḥ paraṃ svayaṃ sākṣātpratyagātmā na cetaraḥ || 216 ||

jāgratsvapnasuṣuptiṣu sphuṭataraṃ yo'sau samujjṛmbhate
pratyagrūpatayā sadāhamahamityantaḥ sphurannaikadhā |
nānākāravikārabhāgina imān paśyannahaṃdhīmukhān
nityānandacidātmanā sphurati taṃ viddhi svametaṃ hṛdi || 217 ||

209 The pleasure level cannot be the true self either, since it is changeable, a conditioned phenomenon, the result of good deeds, and involved in the other levels of consciousness as well.

210 When all these five levels have been disposed of by meditating on scripture, when everything as been eliminated there remains the witness, pure consciousness itself.

211 This self, the light itself, beyond the five levels, the witness of the three states, changeless, unsullied, eternal joy—this should be recognized by the wise as one's real self.

The disciple said:

212 After transcending these five levels as unreal, master, I find nothing but a nothingness, the absence of everything. What object remains for a wise person to identify with?

The teacher said:

213–14 You have spoken the truth, learned one. You are skilled in discrimination. That by which all other phenomena, starting with the thought of "me", are experienced, but which is itself experienced by none, know that, by the subtlest of understanding, as your true self.

215 Whatever is experienced by something else has that as its witness. When there is nothing else to experience something, one cannot talk of it being witnessed.

216 This has the nature of self-awareness, since it is conscious of itself. Thus the individual self is by its self-awareness none other than the Supreme itself.

217 That which is fully manifest in the waking state, dream and deep sleep, which is perceived within in the form of the various experiences and impressions like self-consciousness, and which is experienced as the eternal Bliss, and Consciousness of one's true self, see this within your own heart.

ghaṭodake bimbitamarkabimbam
ālokya mūḍho ravimeva manyate |
tathā cidābhāsamupādhisaṃsthaṃ
bhrāntyāhamityeva jaḍo'bhimanyate || 218 ||

ghaṭaṃ jalaṃ tadgatamarkabimbaṃ
vihāya sarvaṃ vinirīkṣyate'rkaḥ |
taṭastha etattritayāvabhāsakaḥ
svayaṃprakāśo viduṣā yathā tathā || 219 ||

dehaṃ dhiyaṃ citpratibimbamevaṃ
visṛjya buddhau nihitaṃ guhāyām |
draṣṭāramātmānamakhaṇḍabodhaṃ
sarvaprakāśaṃ sadasadvilakṣaṇam || 220 ||
nityaṃ vibhuṃ sarvagataṃ susūkṣmaṃ
antarbahiḥśūnyamananyamātmanaḥ |
vijñāya samyaṅnijarūpametat
pumān vipāpmā virajo vimṛtyuḥ || 221 ||
viśoka ānandaghano vipaścit
svayaṃ kutaścinna bibheti kaścit |
nānyo'sti panthā bhavabandhamukteḥ
vinā svatattvāvagamaṃ mumukṣoḥ || 222 ||

brahmābhinnatvavijñānaṃ bhavamokṣasya kāraṇam |
yenādvitīyamānandaṃ brahma sampadyate budhaiḥ || 223 ||

brahmabhūtastu saṃsṛtyai vidvānnāvartate punaḥ |
vijñātavyamataḥ samyagbrahmābhinnatvamātmanaḥ || 224 ||

satyaṃ jñānamanantaṃ brahma viśuddhaṃ paraṃ svataḥsiddham |
nityānandaikarasaṃ pratyagabhinnaṃ nirantaraṃ jayati || 225 ||

sadidaṃ paramādvaitaṃ svasmādanyasya vastuno'bhāvāt |
na hyanyadasti kiṃcitsamyakparamārthatattvabodhadaśāyām || 226 ||

218 The ignorant see the reflection of the sun in the water of a jar and think it is the sun itself. In the same way the fool sees the reflection of consciousness in its associated qualities and mistakenly identifies himself with it.

219 The wise man ignores jar, water and the sun's reflection in it, and sees the self-illuminating sun itself which gives light to all three but is independent of them.

220–21 When a man abandons the body and the intellect which is just a derivative of consciousness, and recognizing one's true self, the experiencer, pure awareness, the source of everything existent and non-existent, itself devoid of attributes, eternal, all-pervading, omnipresent, subtle, empty of inside and outside, and itself none other than one's true self,[10] he becomes free from evil, sinless and immortal, free from pain, and the incarnation of joy. Master of himself he is afraid of no-one. There is no other way to the breaking of the bonds of temporal existence for the seeker after liberation than the realization of his own true nature.

223 The recognition of one's inseparable oneness with God is the means of liberation from temporal existence, by which the wise person achieves the non-dual, blissful nature of God.

224 Having attained the nature of God, the knower returns no more to the temporal state, so it is essential to recognize one's own true inseparable oneness with God.

225 God is the truth, knowledge and eternal. He is pure, transcendent and self-sufficient—the everlasting, undiluted bliss which is enthroned undivided and inseparable within.

226 This supreme Reality is non-dual in the absence of any other reality beside itself. In the state of knowledge of ultimate truth there is nothing else.

10 for this is truly inborn.

yadidaṃ sakalaṃ viśvaṃ nānārūpaṃ pratītamajñānāt |
tatsarvaṃ brahmaiva pratyastāśeṣabhāvanādoṣam || 227 ||

mṛtkāryabhūto'pi mṛdo na bhinnaḥ
kumbho'sti sarvatra tu mṛtsvarūpāt |
na kumbharūpaṃ pṛthagasti kumbhaḥ
kuto mṛṣā kalpitanāmamātraḥ || 228 ||

kenāpi mṛdbhinnatayā svarūpaṃ
ghaṭasya saṃdarśayituṃ na śakyate |
ato ghaṭaḥ kalpita eva mohān
mṛdeva satyaṃ paramārthabhūtam || 229 ||

sadbrahmakāryaṃ sakalaṃ sadevaṃ
tanmātrametanna tato'nyadasti |
astīti yo vakti na tasya moho
vinirgato nidritavatprajalpaḥ || 230 ||

brahmaivedaṃ viśvamityeva vāṇī
śrautī brūte'tharvaniṣṭhā variṣṭhā |
tasmādetadbrahmamātraṃ hi viśvaṃ
nādhiṣṭhānādbhinnatāropitasya || 231 ||

satyaṃ yadi syājjagadetadātmano
'nantattvahānirnigamāpramāṇatā |
asatyavāditvamapīśituḥ syān
naitattrayaṃ sādhu hitaṃ mahātmanām || 232 ||

īśvaro vastutattvajño na cāhaṃ teṣvavasthitaḥ |
na ca matsthāni bhūtānītyevameva vyacīkḷpat || 233 ||

yadi satyaṃ bhavedviśvaṃ suṣuptāmupalabhyatām |
yannopalabhyate kiṃcidato'satsvapnavanmṛṣā || 234 ||

ataḥ pṛthaṅnāsti jagatparātmanaḥ
pṛthakpratītistu mṛṣā guṇādivat |
āropitasyāsti kimarthavattād
dhiṣṭhānamābhāti tathā bhrameṇa || 235 ||

227 This great variety of things which we experience through our failure to understand is all really God himself, once the distortion of thought is removed.

228 A pot made of clay is nothing other than clay, and its true reality is always simply clay. The pot is no more than the shape of a pot, and is just a mistake of imagination based on the name.

229 No one can show that the reality of the pot is different from the clay, so the pot is just an imagination based on misunderstanding, and the clay is the only final reality.

230 Similarly everything which is made of God is just God and has no separate existence. Whoever says it exists is not yet free from delusion and is like someone talking in his sleep.

231 The supreme scripture of the Arthava Veda declares that "All this is God", so all this is simply God, and anything in addition to that has no reality.

232 If it has any reality, that is the end of any eternal reality for oneself, the scriptures are false, and the Lord himself a liar, three things which are quite unacceptable to great souls.

233 The Lord, who knows the reality of things, has stated "I do not depend on them"[11] and "Things do not exist in me".[12]

234 If everything really existed, it ought to exist in deep sleep too. Since nothing does, then it follows that it is unreal and an illusion like a dream.

235 So the world is not distinct from the Supreme Self, and its perception is an illusion like all attributes. What we add to That has no reality, but merely appears to exist in addition to That through misunderstanding.

11 Bhagavad Gita 9.4.
12 Bhagavad Gita 9.5.

bhrāntasya yadyadbhramataḥ pratītaṃ
bhrāmaiva tattadrajataṃ hi śuktiḥ |
idaṃtayā brahma sadaiva rūpyate
tvāropitaṃ brahmaṇi nāmamātram || 236 ||

ataḥ paraṃ brahma sadadvitīyaṃ
viśuddhavijñānaghanaṃ nirañjanam |
prāśāntamādyantavihīnamakriyaṃ
nirantarānandarasasvarūpam || 237 ||
nirastamāyākṛtasarvabhedaṃ
nityaṃ sukhaṃ niṣkalamaprameyam |
arūpamavyaktamanākhyamavyayaṃ
jyotiḥ svayaṃ kiṃcididaṃ cakāsti || 238 ||

jñātṛjñeyajñānaśūnyamanantaṃ nirvikalpakam |
kevalākhaṇḍacinmātraṃ paraṃ tattvaṃ vidurbudhāḥ || 239 ||

aheyamanupādeyaṃ manovācāmagocaram |
aprameyamanādyantaṃ brahma pūrṇamahaṃ mahaḥ || 240 ||

tattvaṃpadābhyāmabhidhīyamānayoḥ
brahmātmanoḥ śodhitayoryadīttham |
śrutyā tayostattvamasīti samyag
ekatvameva pratipādyate muhuḥ || 241 ||
aikyaṃ tayorlakṣitayorna vācyayoḥ
nigadyate'nyonyaviruddhadharmiṇoḥ |
khadyotabhānvoriva rājabhṛtyayoḥ
kūpāmburāśyoḥ paramāṇumervoḥ || 242 ||

tayorvirodho'yamupādhikalpito
na vāstavaḥ kaścidupādhireṣaḥ |
īśasya māyā mahadādikāraṇaṃ
jīvasya kāryaṃ śṛṇu pañcakośam || 243 ||

etāvupādhī parajīvayostayoḥ
samyaṅnirāse na paro na jīvaḥ |
rājyaṃ narendrasya bhaṭasya kheṭak
tayorapohe na bhaṭo na rājā || 244 ||

236 Whatever a deluded person experiences in his delusion is still always God. The silver is only mother-of-pearl. It is always God that is mistaken for something else, and whatever is added to God is just a name.

237–38 So there exists only the supreme God, the One Reality without a second, consisting of pure consciousness, without any blemish, peace itself and without beginning or end, actionless and having the nature of pure bliss.
Beyond all delusion-created distinctions, this Whatever shines by its own light, eternal, fulfilled, indivisible, infinite, formless, inexpressible, nameless and indestructible.

239 Seers know this supreme Reality, free from the distinctions of knower, known and knowledge, infinite, complete in itself and consisting of pure Awareness.

240 What cannot be got rid of or taken hold of, beyond the sphere of mind and speech, measureless and beginning-and-endless is God, one's true self and supreme glory.

241–42 The words "God" and "yourself", referred to by the terms "That" and "Thou" are conscientiously purified by repetition of the scriptural phrase "Thou art That", and are clearly seen to be identical.
Their identity can be indicated but not described, since they have mutually exclusive meanings like a firefly and the sun, a king and a slave, a well and the ocean, or an atom and mount Meru.

243 The distinction between them is due to the imagined additional associations, but in reality there are no such additions. The primary mental activity is due to the Lord's Māyā, and in the case of the individual it is the result of the five sheaths.

244 These are additions to the Lord and the individual, and when they are removed, there is neither Supreme nor individual. A ruler is known by his kingdom, and a warrior by his arms. Take these away, and there is neither warrior nor king.

athāta ādeśa iti śrutiḥ svayaṃ
niṣedhati brahmaṇi kalpitaṃ dvayam |
śrutipramāṇānugṛhītabodhāt
tayornirāsaḥ karaṇīya eva || 245 ||

nedaṃ nedaṃ kalpitatvānna satyaṃ
rajjudṛṣṭavyālavatsvapnavacca |
itthaṃ dṛśyaṃ sādhuyuktyā vyapohya
jñeyaḥ paścādekabhāvastayoryaḥ || 246 ||

tatastu tau lakṣaṇayā sulakṣyau
tayorakhaṇḍaikarasatvasiddhaye |
nālaṃ jahatyā na tathājahatyā
kintūbhayārthātmikayaiva bhāvyam || 247 ||

sa devadatto'yamitīha caikatā
viruddhadharmāṃśamapāsya kathyate |
yathā tathā tattvamasītivākye
viruddhadharmānubhayatra hitvā || 248 ||
saṃlakṣya cinmātratayā sadātmanoḥ
akhaṇḍabhāvaḥ paricīyate budhaiḥ |
evaṃ mahāvākyaśatena kathyate
brahmātmanoraikyamakhaṇḍabhāvaḥ || 249 ||

asthūlamityetadasannirasya
siddhaṃ svato vyomavadapratarkyam |
ato mṛṣāmātramidaṃ pratītaṃ
jahīhi yatsvātmatayā gṛhītam
brahmāhamityeva viśuddhabuddhyā
viddhi svamātmānamakhaṇḍabodham || 250 ||

mṛtkāryaṃ sakalaṃ ghaṭādi satataṃ mṛnmātramevāhitaṃ
tadvatsajjanitaṃ sadātmakamidaṃ sanmātramevākhilam |
yasmānnāsti sataḥ paraṃ kimapi tatsatyaṃ sa ātmā svayaṃ
tasmāttattvamasi praśāntamamalaṃ brahmādvayaṃ yatparam || 251 ||

245 Scripture itself, with the words "Here is the teaching",[13] denies the imagined duality in God. One must get rid of these additions by means of understanding backed up by the authority of the scriptures.

246 "Not this, not this"[14] means that nothing one can think of is real, like a rope mistaken for a snake, or like a dream. Carefully getting rid of the apparent in this way, one should then come to understand the oneness of the Lord and the individual.

247 So the meaning of these two expressions, Lord and individual, must be carefully considered until their essential oneness is understood. It is not enough just to reject or accept either of them. One must come to the recognition of the identity of the meaning of them both.

248–49 In the phrase "this person is Devadatta" the identity is indicated by removing the distinction, and in the same way, in the expression "Thou art That" the wise must get rid of the apparent contradiction and recognize the complete identity of God and self by carefully identifying the shared attribute of pure consciousness. Hundreds of scriptural sayings declare the identity of oneself and God in this way.

250 In accordance with "It is nothing material"[15] eliminate the unreal and find that which like the sky is pure and solitary, and is beyond thought. Eliminate too this purely illusory body which you have hitherto identified with yourself. Then recognizing, "I am God" with purified understanding, see your true self as undifferentiated consciousness.

251 Everything made of clay, such as pot, is always to be seen as purely clay. In the same way, everything deriving from this supreme Self must be simply recognized as pure Reality. Since there is no reality beyond that, it is truly one's very self, and you are that still, unblemished, non-dual, supreme Reality of God.

13 Brihadaranyaka Upanishad 2.3.6.

14 Brihadaranyaka Upanishad 2.3.6.

15 Brihadaranyaka Upanishad 3.8.8.

nidrākalpitadeśakālaviṣayajñātrādi sarvaṃ yathā
mithyā tadvadihāpi jāgrati jagatsvājñānakāryatvataḥ |
yasmādevamidaṃ śarīrakaraṇaprāṇāhamādyapyasat
tasmāttattvamasi praśāntamamalaṃ brahmādvayaṃ yatparam || 252 ||

yatra bhrāntyā kalpita tadviveke
tattanmātraṃ naiva tasmādvibhinnam |
svapne naṣṭaṃ svapnaviśvaṃ vicitraṃ
svasmādbhinnaṃ kinnu dṛṣṭaṃ prabodhe || 253 ||

jātinītikulagotradūragaṃ
nāmarūpaguṇadoṣavarjitam |
deśakālaviṣayātivarti yad
brahma tattvamasi bhāvayātmani || 254 ||

yatparaṃ sakalavāgagocaraṃ
gocaraṃ vimalabodhacakṣuṣaḥ |
śuddhacidghanamanādi vastu yad
brahma tattvamasi bhāvayātmani || 255 ||

ṣaḍbhirūrmibhirayogi yogihṛd
bhāvitaṃ na karaṇairvibhāvitam |
buddhyavedyamanavadyamasti yad
brahma tattvamasi bhāvayātmani || 256 ||

bhrāntikalpitajagatkalāśrayaṃ
svāśrayaṃ ca sadasadvilakṣaṇam |
niṣkalaṃ nirupamānavaddhi yad
brahma tattvamasi bhāvayātmani || 257 ||

janmavṛddhipariṇatyapakṣaya
vyādhināśanavihīnamavyayam |
viśvasṛṣṭyavavighātakāraṇaṃ
brahma tattvamasi bhāvayātmani || 258 ||

astabhedamanapāstalakṣaṇaṃ
nistaraṅgajalarāśiniścalam |
nityamuktamavibhaktamūrti yad
brahma tattvamasi bhāvayātmani || 259 ||

252 Just as the things like places, time, objects and observer imagined in a dream are unreal, so the world experienced in the waking state too is created by one's own ignorance. Since the body-creating forces, self-identification, and so on, are also unreal, you are that still, unblemished, non-dual, supreme Reality of God.

253 That which is mistakenly imagined to exist is recognized by wisdom to be That alone, and is thus undifferentiated. The colourful world of a dream disappears. What remains other than oneself on waking?

254 Beyond birth, creed, family and tribe, free from the distortion of attributes of name and appearance, transcending locality, time and objects, you are That, God himself. Meditate on the fact within yourself.

255 That supreme Reality beyond the realm of anything that can be said, but the resort of the pure eye of understanding, the pure reality of Consciousness-Awareness-Mind, etc.—you are That, God himself. Meditate on the fact within yourself.

256 That which is unaffected by the six afflictions,[16] which is meditated on in the heart of the devotee, unrecognized by the senses, unknown by the intellect—you are That, God himself. Meditate on the fact within yourself.

257 That basis on which the mistakenly imagined world exists, itself dependent on nothing else, devoid of true and false, without parts, and without mental image—you are That, God himself. Meditate on the fact within yourself.

258 That which is indestructible, free from birth, growth, development, decay, illness and death; which is the cause of the creation, maintenance and destruction of everything—you are That, God himself. Meditate on the fact within yourself.

259 Free of parts, of an unchanging quality, undisturbed like a waveless sea, declared to be of an eternally indivisible nature—you are That, God himself. Meditate on the fact within yourself.

16 of aging, death, hunger, thirst, desire, and ignorance.

ekameva sadanekakāraṇaṃ
kāraṇāntaranirāsyakāraṇam |
kāryakāraṇavilakṣaṇaṃ svayaṃ
brahma tattvamasi bhāvayātmani || 260 ||

nirvikalpakamanalpamakṣaraṃ
yatkṣarākṣaravilakṣaṇaṃ param |
nityamavyayasukhaṃ nirañjanaṃ
brahma tattvamasi bhāvayātmani || 261 ||

yadvibhāti sadanekadhā bhramān
nāmarūpaguṇavikriyātmanā |
hemavatsvayamavikriyaṃ sadā
brahma tattvamasi bhāvayātmani || 262 ||

yaccakāstyanaparaṃ parātparaṃ
pratyagekarasamātmalakṣaṇam |
satyacitsukhamanantamavyayaṃ
brahma tattvamasi bhāvayātmani || 263 ||

uktamarthamimamātmani svayaṃ
bhāvayetprathitayuktibhirdhiyā |
saṃśayādirahitaṃ karāmbuvat
tena tattvanigamo bhaviṣyati || 264 ||

saṃbodhamātraṃ pariśuddhatattvaṃ
vijñāya saṅghe nṛpavacca sainye |
tadāśrayaḥ svātmani sarvadā sthito
vilāpaya brahmaṇi viśvajātam || 265 ||

buddhau guhāyāṃ sadasadvilakṣaṇaṃ
brahmāsti satyaṃ paramadvitīyam |
tadātmanā yo'tra vasedguhāyāṃ
punarna tasyāṅgaguhāpraveśaḥ || 266 ||

jñāte vastunyapi balavatī vāsanānādireṣā
kartā bhoktāpyahamiti dṛḍhā yāsya saṃsārahetuḥ |
pratyagdṛṣṭyātmani nivasatā sāpaneyā prayatnān
muktiṃ prāhustadiha munayo vāsanātānavaṃ yat || 267 ||

260 Itself One but the cause of the many, the supreme Cause which does away with all other causes, itself devoid of distinctions of "cause" and "effect"—you are That, God himself. Meditate on the fact within yourself.

261 Without modification, great and unending, the supreme Reality beyond destruction and indestructibility, the eternal unfading, unblemished, fulfilment—you are That, God himself. Meditate on the fact within yourself.

262 That Reality which manifests itself as the many through the illusions of names, shapes, attributes and changes, but which, like gold is always itself unchanged[17]—you are That, God himself. Meditate on the fact within yourself.

263 That, beyond which there is nothing, but which shines beyond everything else, the inner, uniform self-nature of being-consciousness-joy, infinite and eternal—you are That, God himself. Meditate on the fact within yourself.

264 One should meditate within oneself with the mind well controlled on the truth declared here. Then the truth will be disclosed free from doubt, like water in the palm of one's hand.

265 Realizing one's true nature as pure consciousness, one should remain always established in oneself, like a king surrounded by his army, and should redirect all that is back into God.

266 In the cave of the mind, free from attributes of being and not-being, there exists God, the Truth, supreme and without a second. He who by himself dwells in that cave returns no more to a mother's womb.

267 Even when one knows the truth, there still remains the strong, beginningless tendency to think "I am the doer and the reaper of the consequences" which is the cause of samsara. It must be carefully removed by living in the state of observing the truth within oneself. The wise call that removal of this tendency liberation.

17 in different objects.

ahaṃ mameti yo bhāvo dehākṣādāvanātmani |
adhyāso'yaṃ nirastavyo viduṣā svātmaniṣṭhayā || 268 ||

jñātvā svaṃ pratyagātmānaṃ buddhitadvṛttisākṣiṇam |
so'hamityeva sadvṛttyānātmanyātmamatiṃ jahi || 269 ||

lokānuvartanaṃ tyaktvā tyaktvā dehānuvartanam |
śāstrānuvartanaṃ tyaktvā svādhyāsāpanayaṃ kuru || 270 ||

lokavāsanayā jantoḥ śāstravāsanayāpi ca |
dehavāsanayā jñānaṃ yathāvannaiva jāyate || 271 ||

saṃsārakārāgṛhamokṣamicchor
ayomāyāṃ pādanibandhaśṛṅkhalam |
vadanti tajjñāḥ paṭu vāsanātrayaṃ
yo'smādvimuktaḥ samupaiti muktim || 272 ||

jalādisaṃsargavaśātprabhūta
durgandhadhūtāgarudivyavāsanā |
saṃgharṣaṇenaiva vibhāti samyag
vidhūyamāne sati bāhyagandhe || 273 ||

antaḥśritānantadūrantavāsanā
dhūlīviliptā paramātmavāsanā |
prajñātisaṃgharṣaṇato viśuddhā
pratīyate candanagandhavatsphuṭam || 274 ||

anātmavāsanājālaistirobhūtātmavāsanā |
nityātmaniṣṭhayā teṣāṃ nāśe bhāti svayaṃ sphuṭam || 275 ||

yathā yathā pratyagavasthitaṃ manaḥ
tathā tathā muñcati bāhyavāsanām |
niḥśeṣamokṣe sati vāsanānāṃ
ātmānubhūtiḥ pratibandhaśūnyā || 276 ||

268 The tendency to see "me" and "mine" in the body and the senses, which are not oneself must be done way with by the wise by remaining identified with one's true self.

269 Recognizing one's true inner self, the witness of the mind and its operations, and reflecting on the truth of "I am That", get rid of this wrong opinion about oneself.

270 Abandoning the concerns of the world, abandoning concern about the body, and abandoning even concern about scriptures, see to the removal wrong assumptions about yourself.

271 It is owing to people's worldly desires, their desires for scriptures, and their desires concerning their bodies that they do not achieve realization.

272 Those who know about these things call these three desires the iron fetter that binds the feet of those who are seeking escape from the prison-house of samsara. He who is free from them reaches liberation.

273 The beautiful smell of aloe wood which is masked by a bad smell through contamination by water and such things becomes evident again when it is rubbed clean.

274 Desire for one's true self which is veiled by endless internal other desires becomes pure and evident again like the smell of sandalwood through application with wisdom.

275 When the mass of desires for things other than oneself obscuring the contrary desire for one's real self are eliminated by constant self-remembrance, then it discloses itself of its own accord.

276 As the mind becomes more and more inward-turned, it becomes gradually freed from external desires, and when all such desires are fully eliminated self-realization is completely freed from obstruction.

svātmanyeva sadā sthitvā mano naśyati yoginaḥ |
vāsanānāṃ kṣayaścātaḥ svādhyāsāpanayaṃ kuru || 277 ||

tamo dvābhyāṃ rajaḥ sattvātsattvaṃ śuddhena naśyati |
tasmātsattvamavaṣṭabhya svādhyāsāpanayaṃ kuru || 278 ||

prārabdhaṃ puṣyati vapuriti niścitya niścalaḥ |
dhairyamālambya yatnena svādhyāsāpanayaṃ kuru || 279 ||

nāhaṃ jīvaḥ paraṃ brahmetyatadvyāvṛttipūrvakam |
vāsanāvegataḥ prāptasvādhyāsāpanayaṃ kuru || 280 ||

śrutyā yuktyā svānubhūtyā jñātvā sārvātmyamātmanaḥ |
kvacidābhāsataḥ prāptasvādhyāsāpanayaṃ kuru || 281 ||

anādānavisargābhyāmīṣannāsti kriyā muneḥ |
tadekaniṣṭhayā nityaṃ svādhyāsāpanayaṃ kuru || 282 ||

tattvamasyādivākyotthabrahmātmaikatvabodhataḥ |
brahmaṇyātmatvadārḍhyāya svādhyāsāpanayaṃ kuru || 283 ||

ahaṃbhāvasya dehe'sminniḥśeṣavilayāvadhi |
sāvadhānena yuktātmā svādhyāsāpanayaṃ kuru || 284 ||

pratītirjīvajagatoḥ svapnavadbhāti yāvatā |
tāvannirantaraṃ vidvansvādhyāsāpanayaṃ kuru || 285 ||

277 When he is always poised in self-awareness the yogi's thinking mind stops, and the cessation of desires takes place as a result, so see to the removal of all ideas of additions to your true self.

278 Dullness[18] is removed by passion[19] and purity,[20] desire is removed by purity, and purity when itself purified, so establishing yourself in purity, see to the removal of all ideas of additions to your true self.

279 Recognizing that the effects of past conditioning will sustain the body, remain undisturbed and work away hard at seeing to the removal of all ideas of additions to your true self.

280 "I am not the individual life. I am God." Getting rid of all previous misidentifications like this, see to the removal of all ideas of additions to your true self created by the power of desires.

281 Recognizing yourself as the self of everything by the authority of scripture, by reasoning and by personal experience, see to the removal of all ideas of additions to your true self whenever they manifest themselves.

282 The wise man has no business concerning himself with the acquisition or disposal of things, so by adherence to the one reality, see to the removal of all ideas of additions to your true self.

283 Realizing the identity of yourself and God by the help of sayings like "You are That", see to the removal of all ideas of additions to your true self so as to strengthen the adherence of yourself in God.

284 Eliminate completely your self-identification with this body, and with determination see that your mind is devoted to the removal of all ideas of additions to your true self.

285 So long as even a dream-like awareness of yourself as an individual in the world remains, as a wise person persistently see to the removal of all ideas of additions to your true self.

18 tamas.

19 rajas.

20 sattva.

nidrāyā lokavārtāyāḥ śabdāderapi vismṛteḥ |
kvacinnāvasaraṃ dattvā cintayātmānamātmani || 286 ||

mātāpitrormalodbhūtaṃ malamāṃsamāyāṃ vapuḥ |
tyaktvā cāṇḍālavaddūraṃ brahmībhūya kṛtī bhava || 287 ||

ghaṭākāśaṃ mahākāśa ivātmānaṃ parātmani |
vilāpyākhaṇḍabhāvena tūṣṇī bhava sadā mune || 288 ||

svaprakāśamadhiṣṭhānaṃ svayaṃbhūya sadātmanā |
brahmāṇḍamapi piṇḍāṇḍaṃ tyajyatāṃ malabhāṇḍavat || 289 ||

cidātmani sadānande dehārūḍhāmahaṃdhiyam |
niveśya liṅgamutsṛjya kevalo bhava sarvadā || 290 ||

yatraiṣa jagadābhāso darpaṇāntaḥ puraṃ yathā |
tadbrahmāhamiti jñātvā kṛtakṛtyo bhaviṣyasi || 291 ||

yatsatyabhūtaṃ nijarūpamādyaṃ
cidadvayānandamarūpamakriyam |
tadetya mithyāvapurutsṛjeta
śailūṣavadveṣamupāttamātmanaḥ || 292 ||

sarvātmanā dṛśyamidaṃ mṛṣaiva
naivāhamarthaḥ kṣaṇikatvadarśanāt |
jānāmyahaṃ sarvamiti pratītiḥ
kuto'hamādeḥ kṣaṇikasya sidhyet || 293 ||

ahaṃpadārthastvahamādisākṣī
nityaṃ suṣuptāvapi bhāvadarśanāt |
brūte hyajo nitya iti śrutiḥ svayaṃ
tatpratyagātmā sadasadvilakṣaṇaḥ || 294 ||

286 Without giving way to the least descent into forgetfulness through sleep, worldly affairs or the various senses, meditate on yourself within.

287 Shunning the body which is derived from the impurities of your mother and father and itself made up of impurities and flesh as you would an outcaste from a good distance, become Godlike and achieve the goal of life.

288 Restoring the self in you to the supreme Self like the space in a jar back to Space itself by meditation on their indivisibility, always remain silent, wise one.

289 Taking up through your true self the condition of your real glory, reject thoughts of a divine universe as much as of yourself as a reality, as you would a dish of filth.

290 Transferring your present self-identification with the body to yourself as consciousness, being and bliss, abandon the body and be complete forever.

291 When you know "I am that very God" in which the reflection of the world appears, like a city in a mirror, then you will be one who has achieved the goal of life.

292 Attaining that Reality which is self-existent and primal, non-dual consciousness, and bliss, formless and actionless, one should abandon the unreal body taken on by oneself, like an actor doffing his costume.

293 All this experienced by oneself is false, and so is the sense of I-hood in view of its ephemeral nature. How can "I know everything" be true of something which is itself ephemeral.

294 That which warrants the term "I" on the other hand is that which is the observer of the thought "I" etc. in view of its permanent existence even in the state of deep sleep. Scripture itself declares that it is "unborn and eternal".[21] That true inner self is distinct from both being and not-being.

21 Katha Upanishad 1.2.18.

vikāriṇāṃ sarvavikāravettā
nityāvikāro bhavituṃ samarhati |
manorathasvapnasuṣuptiṣu sphuṭaṃ
punaḥ punardṛṣṭamasattvametayoḥ || 295 ||

ato'bhimānaṃ tyaja māṃsapiṇḍe
piṇḍābhimāninyapi buddhikalpite |
kālatrayābādhyamakhaṇḍabodhaṃ
jñātvā svamātmānamupaihi śāntim || 296 ||

tyajābhimānaṃ kulagotranāma
rūpāśrameṣvārdraśavāśriteṣu |
liṅgasya dharmānapi kartṛtādiṃs
tyaktā bhavākhaṇḍasukhasvarūpaḥ || 297 ||

santyanye pratibandhāḥ puṃsaḥ saṃsārahetavo dṛṣṭāḥ |
teṣāmevaṃ mūlaṃ prathamavikāro bhavatyahaṃkāraḥ || 298 ||

yāvatsyātsvasya saṃbandho'haṃkāreṇa durātmanā |
tāvanna leśamātrāpi muktivārtā vilakṣaṇā || 299 ||

ahaṃkāragrahānmuktaḥ svarūpamupapadyate |
candravadvimalaḥ pūrṇaḥ sadānandaḥ svayaṃprabhaḥ || 300 ||

yo vā pure so'hamiti pratīto
buddhyā praklṛptastamasātimūḍhayā |
tasyaiva niḥśeṣatayā vināśe
brahmātmabhāvaḥ pratibandhaśūnyaḥ || 301 ||

brahmānandanidhirmahābalavatāhaṃkāraghorāhinā
saṃveṣṭyātmani rakṣyate guṇamāyāiścaṇḍestribhirmastakaiḥ |
vijñānākhyamahāsinā śrutimatā vicchidya śīrṣatrayaṃ
nirmūlyāhimimaṃ nidhiṃ sukhakaraṃ dhīro'nubhoktuṃkṣamaḥ || 302 ||

yāvadvā yatkiṃcidviṣadoṣasphūrtirasti ceddehe |
kathamārogyāya bhavettadvadahantāpi yogino muktyai || 303 ||

295 The knower of all the changes in changing things must itself be permanent and unchanging. The unreality in the extremes of being and not-being is repeatedly seen in the experience of thought, dreaming and deep sleep.

296 So give up identification with this mass of flesh as well as with what thinks it a mass. Both are intellectual imaginations. Recognize your true self as undifferentiated awareness, unaffected by time, past, present or future, and enter Peace.

297 Give up identification with family, tribe, name, shape and status which depend on the putrid body. Give up physical properties too such as the sense of being the doer and be the very nature of undifferentiated joy.

298 There are other obstacles seen to be the cause of samsara for men. Of these the root and first manifestation is the sense of doership.

299 So long as one has any association with this awful sense of being the doer there cannot be the least achievement of liberation which is something very different.

300 Free from the grasp of feeling oneself the doer, one achieves ones true nature which is, like the moon, pure, consummate, self-illuminating being and bliss.

301 Even he who, with a mind under the influence of strong dullness, has thought of himself as the body, will attain to full identification with God when that delusion is completely removed.

302 The treasure of the bliss of God is coiled round by the very powerful, terrible snake of doership which guards it with its three fierce heads consisting of the three qualities[22] but the wise man can enjoy this bliss-imparting treasure by cutting off the snake's three heads with the great sword of understanding of the scriptures.

303 How can one be free from pain so long as there is there is any trace of poison in the body? The same applies to the pain of self-consciousness in an aspirant's liberation.

22 dullness, passion, and purity.

ahamo'tyantanivṛttyā tatkṛtanānāvikalpasaṃhṛtyā |
pratyaktattvavivekādidamahamasmīti vindate tattvam || 304 ||

ahaṃkāre kartaryahamiti matiṃ muñca sahasā
vikārātmanyātmapratiphalajuṣi svasthitimuṣi |
yadadhyāsātprāptā janimṛtijarāduḥkhabahulā
pratīcaścinmūrtestava sukhatanoḥ saṃsṛtiriyam || 305 ||

sadaikarūpasya cidātmano vibhor
ānandamūrteranavadyakīrteḥ |
naivānyathā kvāpyavikāriṇaste
vināhamadhyāsamamuṣya saṃsṛtiḥ || 306 ||

tasmādahaṃkāramimaṃ svaśatruṃ
bhokturgale kaṇṭakavatpratītam |
vicchidya vijñānamahāsinā sphuṭaṃ
bhuṅkṣvātmasāmrājyasukhaṃ yatheṣṭam || 307 ||

tato'hamādervinivartya vṛttiṃ
saṃtyaktarāgaḥ paramārthalābhāt |
tūṣṇīṃ samāssvātmasukhānubhūtyā
pūrṇātmanā brahmaṇi nirvikalpaḥ || 308 ||

samūlakṛtto'pi mahānahaṃ punaḥ
vyullekhitaḥ syādyadi cetasā kṣaṇam |
saṃjīvya vikṣepaśataṃ karoti
nabhasvatā prāvṛṣi vārido yathā || 309 ||

nigṛhya śatrorahamo'vakāśaḥ
kvacinna deyo viṣayānucintayā |
sa eva saṃjīvanaheturasya
prakṣīṇajambīratarorivāmbu || 310 ||

dehātmanā saṃsthita eva kāmī
vilakṣaṇaḥ kāmayitā kathaṃ syāt |
ato'rthasandhānaparatvameva
bhedaprasaktyā bhavabandhahetuḥ || 311 ||

304 In the total cessation of self-identification and the ending of the multifarious mental misrepresentations it causes, the truth of "This is what I am" is achieved through inner discernment.

305 Get rid forthwith of doership, your self-identification, that is, with the agent, a distorted vision of yourself which stops you from resting in your true nature, and by identification with which you, who are really pure consciousness and a manifestation of joy itself, experience samsara with all its birth, decay, death and suffering.

306 You are really unchanging, the eternally unvarying Lord, consciousness, bliss and indestructible glory. If it were not for the wrong identification with a false self you would not be subject to samsara.

307 So cut down your enemy, this sense of being the doer, with the great sword of knowledge, caught like a splinter in the throat of some-one having a meal, and enjoy to your heart's content the joy of the possession of your true nature.

308 Stop the activity of the false self-identification and so on, get rid of desire by the attainment of the supreme Reality, and practice silence in the experience of the joy of your true self, free from fantasies, with your true nature fulfilled in God.

309 Even when thoroughly eradicated, a great sense of doership can revive again and create a hundred different distractions, if it is once dwelt on again for a moment in the mind, like monsoon rain-clouds driven on by the wind.

310 Overcoming the enemy of the false self, one should give it no opportunity by dwelling on the senses again, because that is the way it comes back to life, like water for a withered citrous tree.

311 He who is attached to the idea of himself as the body is desirous of physical pleasure, but how could some-one devoid of such an idea seek physical pleasure? Hence separation from one's true good is the cause of bondage to samsara since one is stuck in seeing things as separate from oneself.

kāryapravardhanādbījapravṛddhiḥ paridṛśyate |
kāryanāśādbījanāśastasmātkāryaṃ nirodhayet || 312 ||

vāsanāvṛddhitaḥ kāryaṃ kāryavṛddhyā ca vāsanā |
vardhate sarvathā puṃsaḥ saṃsāro na nivartate || 313 ||

saṃsārabandhavicchittyai taddvayaṃ pradahedyatiḥ |
vāsanāvṛddhiretābhyāṃ cintayā kriyayā bahiḥ || 314 ||

tābhyāṃ pravardhamānā sā sūte saṃsṛtimātmanaḥ |
trayāṇāṃ ca kṣayopāyaḥ sarvāvasthāsu sarvadā || 315 ||
sarvatra sarvataḥ sarvabrahmamātrāvalokanaiḥ |
sadbhāvavāsanādārḍhyāttattrayaṃ layamaśnute || 316 ||

kriyānāśe bhaveccintānāśo'smādvāsanākṣayaḥ |
vāsanāprakṣayo mokṣaḥ sā jīvanmuktiriṣyate || 317 ||

sadvāsanāsphūrtivijṛmbhaṇe sati
hyasau vilīnāpyahamādivāsanā |
atiprakṛṣṭāpyaruṇaprabhāyāṃ
vilīyate sādhu yathā tamisrā || 318 ||

tamastamaḥkāryamanarthajālaṃ
na dṛśyate satyudite dineśe |
tathādvayānandarasānubhūtau
na vāsti bandho na ca duḥkhagandhaḥ || 319 ||

dṛśyaṃ pratītaṃ pravilāpayansan
sanmātramānandaghanaṃ vibhāvayan |
samāhitaḥ sanbahirantaraṃ vā
kālaṃ nayethāḥ sati karmabandhe || 320 ||

pramādo brahmaniṣṭhāyāṃ na kartavyaḥ kadācana |
pramādo mṛtyurityāha bhagavānbrahmaṇaḥ sutaḥ || 321 ||

312 A seed is seen to grow with the development of the necessary conditions, while the failure of the conditions leads to the failure of the seed. So one must remove these conditions.

313 The increase of desires leads to activity, and from the increase of activity there is more desire. Thus a man prospers in every way, and samsara never comes to an end.

314 To break the bonds of samsara, the ascetic should burn away both of these,[23] since thinking about these and external activity lead to the increase of desires.

315–16 The increase of these two is the cause of one's samsara, and the means to the destruction of these three is to see everything as simply God everywhere, always and in all circumstances. By the increase of desire for becoming the Truth, these three come to an end.

317 Through the stopping of activity there comes the stopping of thinking, and then the cessation of desires. The cessation of desires is liberation, and is what is known as here-and-now liberation.

318 When the force of the desire for the Truth blossoms, selfish desires wither away, just like darkness vanishes before the radiance of the light of dawn.

319 Darkness and the mass of evils produced by darkness no longer exist when the sun has risen. Similarly, when one has tasted undifferentiated bliss, no bondage or trace of suffering remains.

320 Transcending everything to do with the senses, cultivating the blissful and only Truth, and at peace within and without—this is how one should pass one's time so long as any bonds of karma remain.

321 One should never permit carelessness in one's adherence to God. "Carelessness is death"[24] says the Master[25] who was of Brahma's son.

23 desire and activity.

24 Mahabharata 5.42.43.

na pramādādanartho'nyo jñāninaḥ svasvarūpataḥ |
tato mohastato'haṃdhīstato bandhastato vyathā || 322 ||

viṣayābhimukhaṃ dṛṣṭvā vidvāṃsamapi vismṛtiḥ |
vikṣepayati dhīdoṣairyoṣā jāramiva priyam || 323 ||

yathāpakṛṣṭaṃ śaivālaṃ kṣaṇamātraṃ na tiṣṭhati |
āvṛṇoti tathā māyā prājñaṃ vāpi parāṅmukham || 324 ||

lakṣyacyutaṃ cedyadi cittamīṣad
bahirmukhaṃ sannipatettatastataḥ |
pramādataḥ pracyutakelikandukaḥ
sopānapaṅktau patito yathā tathā || 325 ||

viṣayeṣvāviśaccetaḥ saṃkalpayati tadguṇān |
samyaksaṃkalpanātkāmaḥ kāmātpuṃsaḥ pravartanam || 326 ||

ataḥ pramādānna paro'sti mṛtyuḥ
vivekino brahmavidaḥ samādhau |
samāhitaḥ siddhimupaiti samyak
samāhitātmā bhava sāvadhānaḥ || 327 ||

tataḥ svarūpavibhraṃśo vibhraṣṭastu patatyadhaḥ |
patitasya vinā nāśaṃ punarnāroha īkṣyate || 328 ||

saṃkalpaṃ varjayettasmātsarvānarthasya kāraṇam |
jīvato yasya kaivalyaṃ videhe sa ca kevalaḥ
yatkiṃcitpaśyato bhedaṃ bhayaṃ brūte yajuḥśrutiḥ || 329 ||

yadā kadā vāpi vipaścideṣa
brahmaṇyanante'pyaṇumātrabhedam |
paśyatyathāmuṣya bhayaṃ tadaiva
yadvīkṣitaṃ bhinnatayā pramādāt || 330 ||

322 There is no greater evil than carelessness about his own true nature for a wise man. From this comes delusion, from this comes misconceptions about oneself, from this comes bondage, from this comes suffering.

323 Forgetfulness afflicts even a wise man with harmful mental states when it finds him well-disposed to the senses, like a woman does her infatuated lover.

324 Just as the algae cleared off water does not stay off even for a moment, so illusion obscures the sight of even a wise man whose mind is outward-directed.

325 When the mind loses its direction towards its goal and becomes outward-turned it runs from one thing to another, like a play-ball carelessly dropped on the steps of some stairs.

326 A mind directed towards the senses dwells with imagination on their qualities. From imagining finally comes desire, and from desire comes the way a man directs his activity.

327 As a result, there is no death like carelessness in meditation to the wise knower of God. The meditator achieves perfect fulfilment, so carefully practice peace of mind.

328[26] From carelessness one turns aside from one's true nature, and he who turns aside from it slips downwards. He who has thus fallen invariably comes to disaster, but is not seen to rise again.

329 So one should abandon the imagination which is the cause of all ills. He has reached fulfilment who is completely dead while still alive. The Yajur Veda[27] declares there is still something to fear for anyone who still sees distinctions in things.

330 Whenever a wise man sees the least distinction in the infinite God, whatever he has carelessly perceived as a distinction then becomes a source of fear for him.

25 Sanatkumara.

26 See the note on page 138 below.

27 Taittiriya Upanishad 2.7.

śrutismṛtinyāyaśatairniṣiddhe
dṛśye'tra yaḥ svātmamatiṃ karoti |
upaiti duḥkhopari duḥkhajātaṃ
niṣiddhakartā sa malimluco yathā || 331 ||

satyābhisaṃdhānarato vimukto
mahattvamātmīyamupaiti nityam |
mithyābhisandhānaratastu naśyed
dṛṣṭaṃ tadetadyadacauracaurayoḥ || 332 ||

yatirasadanusandhiṃ bandhahetuṃ vihāya
svayamāyāmahamasmītyātmadṛṣṭyaiva tiṣṭhet |
sukhayati nanu niṣṭhā brahmaṇi svānubhūtyā
harati paramavidyākāryaduḥkhaṃ pratītam || 333 ||

bāhyānusandhiḥ parivardhayetphalaṃ
durvāsanāmeva tatastato'dhikām |
jñātvā vivekaiḥ parihṛtya bāhyaṃ
svātmānusandhiṃ vidadhīta nityam || 334 ||

bāhye niruddhe manasaḥ prasannatā
manaḥprasāde paramātmadarśanam |
tasminsudṛṣṭe bhavabandhanāśo
bahirnirodhaḥ padavī vimukteḥ || 335 ||

kaḥ paṇḍitaḥ sansadasadvivekī
śrutipramāṇaḥ paramārthadarśī |
jānanhi kuryādasato'valambaṃ
svapātahetoḥ śiśuvanmumukṣuḥ || 336 ||

dehādisaṃsaktimato na muktiḥ
muktasya dehādyabhimatyabhāvaḥ |
suptasya no jāgaraṇaṃ na jāgrataḥ
svapnastayorbhinnaguṇāśrayatvāt || 337 ||

331 When, in spite of hundreds of testimonies to the contrary in the Vedas and other scriptures, one identifies oneself with anything to do with the senses, one experiences countless sorrows, doing something prohibited like a thief.

332 He who is devoted to meditating on the Truth attains the eternal glory of his true nature, while he who delights in dwelling on the unreal perishes. This can be seen even in the case of whether someone is a thief or not.

333 An ascetic should abandon dwelling on the unreal which is the cause of bondage, and should fix his attention on himself in his knowledge that "This is what I am". Establishment in God through self-awareness leads to joy and finally removes the suffering caused by ignorance.

334 Dwelling on externals increases the fruit of superfluous evil desires for all sorts of things, so wisely recognizing this fact, one should abandon externals and cultivate attention to one's true nature within.

335 When externals are abandoned there comes peace of mind. When the mind is at peace there comes awareness of one's supreme self. When that is fully experienced there comes the destruction of the bonds of samsara, so abandonment of externals is the road to liberation.

336 What man, being learned, and aware of the distinction between real and unreal, relying on the scriptures and seeking the supreme goal of life, would knowingly, like a child, hanker after resting in the unreal, the cause of his own downfall.

337 There is no liberation for him who is deliberately attached to the body and such things, while there is no self-identification with such things as the body for a liberated man. There is no being awake for some-one asleep, nor sleep for some-one awake, for these two states are by their very nature distinct.

antarbahiḥ svaṃ sthirajaṅgameṣu
jñātvātmanādhāratayā vilokya |
tyaktākhilopādhirakhaṇḍarūpaḥ
pūrṇātmanā yaḥ sthita eṣa muktaḥ || 338 ||

sarvātmanā bandhavimuktihetuḥ
sarvātmabhāvānna paro'sti kaścit |
dṛśyāgrahe satyupapadyate'sau
sarvātmabhāvo'sya sadātmaniṣṭhayā || 339 ||

dṛśyasyāgrahaṇaṃ kathaṃ nu ghaṭate dehātmanā tiṣṭhato
bāhyārthānubhavaprasaktamanasastattatkriyāṃ kurvataḥ |
saṃnyastākhiladharmakarmaviṣayairnityātmaniṣṭhāparaiḥ
tattvajñaiḥ karaṇīyamātmani sadānandecchubhiryatnataḥ || 340 ||

sarvātmasiddhaye bhikṣoḥ kṛtaśravaṇakarmaṇaḥ |
samādhiṃ vidadhātyeṣā śānto dānta iti śrutiḥ || 341 ||

ārūḍhaśakterahamo vināśaḥ
kartunna śakya sahasāpi paṇḍitaiḥ |
ye nirvikalpākhyasamādhiniścalāḥ
tānantarānantabhavā hi vāsanāḥ || 342 ||

ahaṃbuddhyaiva mohinyā yojayitvāvṛterbalāt |
vikṣepaśaktiḥ puruṣaṃ vikṣepayati tadguṇaiḥ || 343 ||

vikṣepaśaktivijayo viṣamo vidhātuṃ
niḥśeṣamāvaraṇaśaktinivṛttyabhāve |
dṛgdṛśyayoḥ sphuṭapayojalavadvibhāge
naśyettadāvaraṇamātmani ca svabhāvāt
niḥsaṃśayena bhavati pratibandhaśūnyo
vikṣepaṇaṃ nahiṃ tadā yadi cenmṛṣārthe || 344 ||

338 He who knows himself within and without, and recognizes himself as the underlying support in all things moving and unmoving, remaining indivisible, fulfilled in himself by abandoning all that is not himself—he is liberated.

339 The means of liberation from bondage is through the one self in everything, and there is nothing higher than this one self in everything. When one does not cling to anything to do with the senses, one achieves these things, and being the one self in everything depends on resting in one's true self.

340 How is not clinging to the senses possible when one's basis is self-identification with the body, and one's mind is attached to enjoying external pleasures, and on doing whatever is necessary to do so? But it can be achieved within themselves by those who have abandoned all objects of rules and observances, who are always resting in self-awareness, who know the Truth and energetically seek the bliss of Reality.

341 Scripture prescribes meditation for realization of the self in everything to the ascetic who has fulfilled the requirement of listening to scripture, saying "At peace and self-controlled" and so on.[28]

342 Even wise men cannot get rid of the sense of doership all of a sudden when it has grown strong, but those who are unwavering in so-called imageless samadhi can, whose desire for this has been developed over countless lives.

343 The outward-turning power of the mind binds a man to the sense of doership by its veiling effect, and confuses him by the attributes of that power.

344 To overcome the outward-turning power of the mind is hard to accomplish without completely eliminating the veiling effect, but the covering over one's inner self can be removed by discriminating between seer and objects, like between milk and water. Absence of an barrier is finally unquestionable when there is no longer any distraction caused by illusory objects.

28 Brihadaranyaka Upanishad 4.4.23.

samyagvivekaḥ sphuṭabodhajanyo
vibhajya dṛgdṛśyapadārthatattvam |
chinatti māyākṛtamohabandhaṃ
yasmādvimuktastu punarna saṃsṛtiḥ || 345 ||

parāvaraikatvavivekavanhiḥ
dahatyavidyāgahanaṃ hyaśeṣam |
kiṃ syātpunaḥ saṃsaraṇasya bījaṃ
advaitabhāvaṃ samupeyuṣo'sya || 346 ||

āvaraṇasya nivṛttirbhavati hi samyakpadārthadarśanataḥ |
mithyājñānavināśastadvikṣepajanitaduḥkhanivṛttiḥ || 347 ||

etattritayaṃ dṛṣṭaṃ samyagrajjusvarūpavijñānāt |
tasmādvastusatattvaṃ jñātavyaṃ bandhamuktaye viduṣā || 348 ||

ayo'gniyogādiva satsamanvayān
mātrādirūpeṇa vijṛmbhate dhīḥ |
tatkāryametaddvitayaṃ yato mṛṣā
dṛṣṭaṃ bhramasvapnamanorathesu || 349 ||
tato vikārāḥ prakṛterahaṃmukhā
dehāvasānā viṣayāśca sarve |
kṣaṇe'nyathābhāvitayā hyamīṣām
asattvamātmā tu kadāpi nānyathā || 350 ||

nityādvayākhaṇḍacidekarūpo
buddhyādisākṣī sadasadvilakṣaṇaḥ |
ahaṃpadapratyayalakṣitārthaḥ
pratyaksadānandaghanaḥ parātmā || 351 ||

itthaṃ vipaścitsadasadvibhajya
niścitya tattvaṃ nijabodhadṛṣṭyā |
jñātvā svamātmānamakhaṇḍabodhaṃ
tebhyo vimuktaḥ svayameva śāmyati || 352 ||

345 Perfect discrimination, born of direct experience establishing the truth of the distinction between seer and objects, severs the bonds of delusion produced by Māyā,[29] \][[and as a result the liberated person is no longer subject to samsara.

346 The fire of the knowledge of the oneness of above and below burns up completely the tangled forest of ignorance. What seed of samsara could there still be for such a person who has achieved non-duality?

347 The veiling effect only disappears with full experience of Reality, and the elimination of false knowledge leads to the end of the suffering caused by that distraction.

348 These three[30] are clearly apparent in the case of recognizing the true nature of the rope, so a wise man should get to know the truth about the underlying reality if he wants to be liberated from his bonds.

349–50 Like fire in conjunction with iron, the mind manifests itself as knower and objects by dependence on something real, but as the duality that causes is seen to be unreal in the case of delusions, dreams and fantasies, so the products of natural causation, from the idea of doership down to the body itself and all its senses, are also unreal in view of the way they are changing every moment, while one's true nature itself never changes.

351 The supreme self is the internal reality of Truth and Bliss, eternally indivisible and pure consciousness, the witness of the intellect and the other faculties, distinct from being or not-being, the reality implied by the word "I".

352 Distinguishing the real from the unreal in this way by means of his inborn capacity of understanding, and liberated from these bonds, a wise man attains peace by recognizing his own true nature as undifferentiated awareness.

29 the creative power, which makes things appear to exist.
30 the removal of veiling effect, false knowledge and suffering.

ajñānahṛdayagranthernihśeṣavilayastadā |
samādhināvikalpena yadādvaitātmadarśanam || 353 ||

tvamahamidamitīyaṃ kalpanā buddhidoṣāt
prabhavati paramātmanyadvaye nirviśeṣe |
pravilasati samādhāvasya sarvo vikalpo
vilayanamupagacchedvastutattvāvadhṛtyā || 354 ||

śānto dāntaḥ paramuparataḥ kṣāntiyuktaḥ samādhiṃ
kurvannityaṃ kalayati yatiḥ svasya sarvātmabhāvam |
tenāvidyātimirajanitānsādhu dagdhvā vikalpān
brahmākṛtyā nivasati sukhaṃ niṣkriyo nirvikalpaḥ || 355 ||

samāhitā ye pravilāpya bāhyaṃ
śrotrādi cetaḥ svamahaṃ cidātmani |
ta eva muktā bhavapāśabandhaiḥ
nānye tu pārokṣyakathābhidhāyinaḥ || 356 ||

upādhibhedātsvayameva bhidyate
copādhyapohe svayameva kevalaḥ |
tasmādupādhervilayāya vidvān
vasetsadākalpasamādhiniṣṭhayā || 357 ||

sati sakto naro yāti sadbhāvaṃ hyekaniṣṭhayā |
kīṭako bhramaraṃ dhyāyan bhramaratvāya kalpate || 358 ||

kriyāntarāsaktimapāsya kīṭako
dhyāyannalitvaṃ hyalibhāvamṛcchati |
tathaiva yogī paramātmatattvaṃ
dhyātvā samāyāti tadekaniṣṭhayā || 359 ||

atīva sūkṣmaṃ paramātmatattvaṃ
na sthūladṛṣṭyā pratipattumarhati |
samādhinātyantasusūkṣmavṛtyā
jñātavyamāryairatiśuddhabuddhibhiḥ || 360 ||

353 The knot of ignorance in the heart is finally removed when one comes to see one's own true non-dual nature by means of imageless samadhi.

354 Assumptions of "you", "me", "it" occur in the non-dual, undifferentiated supreme self because of a failure in the understanding, but all a man's false assumptions disappear in samadhi and are completely destroyed by the realization of the truth of the underlying reality.

355 An ascetic who is peaceful, disciplined, fully withdrawn, long-suffering and meditative always cultivates the presence of the self of everything in himself. Eradicating in this way the false assumptions created by the distorting vision of ignorance, he lives happily in God free from action and free from imaginations.

356 Only those who have achieved samadhi and who have withdrawn the external senses, the mind and their sense of doership into their true nature as consciousness are free from being trapped in the snare of samsara, not those who just repeat the statements of others.

357 Because of the diversity of the things he identifies himself with, a man tends to see himself as complex, but with the removal of the identification, he is himself again and perfect as he is. For this reason a wise man should get rid of self-identifications and always cultivate imageless samadhi.

358 Adhering to the Real a man comes to share in the nature of that Reality by his one-pointed concentration on it, in the same way that a grub is able to become a wasp by concentration on a wasp.

359 A grub achieves wasphood by abandoning attachment to other activities and concentrating on the nature of being a wasp. In the same way an ascetic meditates on the reality of the supreme self and achieves it through his one-pointed concentration on it.

360 The reality of the supreme self is extremely subtle and is not capable of being experienced by those of coarse vision, but it can be known by those worthy of it by reason of their very pure understanding by means of a mind made extremely subtle by meditation.

yathā suvarṇaṃ puṭapākaśodhitaṃ
tyaktvā malaṃ svātmaguṇaṃ samṛcchati |
tathā manaḥ sattvarajastamomalaṃ
dhyānena santyajya sameti tattvam || 361 ||

nirantarābhyāsavaśāttaditthaṃ
pakvaṃ mano brahmaṇi līyate yadā |
tadā samādhiḥ savikalpavarjitaḥ
svato'dvayānandarasānubhāvakaḥ || 362 ||

samādhinānena samastavāsanā
granthervināśo'khilakarmanāśaḥ |
antarbahiḥ sarvata eva sarvadā
svarūpavisphūrtirayatnataḥ syāt || 363 ||

śruteḥ śataguṇaṃ vidyānmananaṃ mananādapi |
nidiṃdhyāsaṃ lakṣaguṇamanantaṃ nirvikalpakam || 364 ||

nirvikalpakasamādhinā sphuṭaṃ
brahmatattvamavagamyate dhruvam |
nānyathā calatayā manogateḥ
pratyayāntaravimiśritaṃ bhavet || 365 ||

ataḥ samādhatsva yatendriyaḥ san
nirantaraṃ śāntamanāḥ pratīci |
vidhvaṃsaya dhvāntamanādyavidyayā
kṛtaṃ sadekatvavilokanena || 366 ||

yogasya prathamadvāraṃ vāṅnirodho'parigrahaḥ |
nirāśā ca nirīhā ca nityamekāntaśīlatā || 367 ||

ekāntasthitirindriyoparamaṇe henurdamaścetasaḥ
saṃrodhe karaṇaṃ śamena vilayaṃ yāyādahaṃvāsanā |
tenānandarasānubhūtiracalā brāhmī sadā yoginaḥ
tasmāccittanirodha eva satataṃ kāryaḥ prayatno muneḥ || 368 ||

361 As gold purified in a furnace loses its impurities and achieves its own true nature, the mind gets rid of the impurities of the attributes of delusion, passion and purity through meditation and attains Reality.

362 When by the effect of constant meditation the purified mind becomes one with God, then samadhi, now freed from images, experiences in itself the state of non-dual bliss.

363 The destruction of the bonds of all desires through this samadhi is the destruction of all karma, and there follows the manifestation of one's true nature without effort, inside, outside, everywhere and always.

364 Thought should be considered a hundred times better than hearing, and meditation is thousands of times better than thought, while imageless samadhi is infinite in its effect.

365 The experience of the reality of God becomes permanent though imageless samadhi, but not otherwise as it is mixed with other things by the restlessness of the mind.

366 So, established in meditation, with the senses controlled, the mind calmed and continually turned inwards, destroy the darkness of beginningless ignorance by recognizing the oneness of Reality.

367 The primary door to union with God is cutting off talking, not accepting possessions, freedom from expectation, dispassion and a secluded manner of life.

368 Living in seclusion is the cause of control of the senses, restraint of the mind leads to inner stillness and tranquillity leads to mastery of self-centred desire. From that comes the ascetic's continual experience of the unbroken bliss of God. So the wise man should always strive for the cessation of thought.

vācaṃ niyacchātmani taṃ niyaccha
buddhau dhiyaṃ yaccha ca buddhisākṣiṇi |
taṃ cāpi pūrṇātmani nirvikalpe
vilāpya śāntiṃ paramāṃ bhajasva || 369 ||

dehaprāṇendriyamanobuddhyādibhirupādhibhiḥ |
yairyairvṛtteḥsamāyogastatadbhāvo'sya yoginaḥ || 370 ||

tannivṛttyā muneḥ samyaksarvoparamaṇaṃ sukham |
saṃdṛśyate sadānandarasānubhavaviplavaḥ || 371 ||

antastyāgo bahistyāgo viraktasyaiva yujyate |
tyajatyantarbahiḥsaṅgaṃ viraktastu mumukṣayā || 372 ||

bahistu viṣayaiḥ saṅgaṃ tathāntarahamādibhiḥ |
virakta eva śaknoti tyaktuṃ brahmaṇi niṣṭhitaḥ || 373 ||

vairāgyabodhau puruṣasya pakṣivat
pakṣau vijānīhi vicakṣaṇa tvam |
vimuktisaudhāgralatādhirohaṇaṃ
tābhyāṃ vinā nānyatareṇa sidhyati || 374 ||

atyantavairāgyavataḥ samādhiḥ
samāhitasyaiva dṛḍhaprabodhaḥ |
prabuddhatattvasya hi bandhamuktiḥ
muktātmano nityasukhānubhūtiḥ || 375 ||

vairāgyānna paraṃ sukhasya janakaṃ paśyāmi vaśyātmanaḥ
taccecchuddhatarātmabodhasahitaṃ svārājyasāmrājyadhuk |
etaddvāramajasramuktiyuvateryasmāttvamasmātparaṃ
sarvatrāspṛhayā sadātmani sadā prajñāṃ kuru śreyase || 376 ||

369 Restrain speech within. Restrain the mind in the understanding and restrain the understanding in the consciousness that observes the understanding. Restrain that in the perfect and imageless self, and enjoy supreme peace.

370 Body, functions, senses, mind, understanding and so on—whichever of these adjuncts the mind's activity is connected with, that becomes the ascetic's identity for the time.

371 When this process is stopped, the wise man knows the perfect joy of the letting go of everything, and experiences the attainment of the overwhelming bliss of Reality.

372 Internal renunciation and external renunciation—it is the dispassionate man who is capable of these. The dispassionate man abandons fetters internal and external because of his yearning for liberation.

373 The dispassionate man, established in God, is indeed capable of abandoning the external bond of the senses and the internal one of selfishness and so on.

374 As a discriminating person realize that dispassion and understanding are like a bird's wings for a man. Without them both he cannot reach the nectar of liberation growing on top of a creeper.

375 The extremely dispassionate man achieves samadhi. A person in samadhi experiences steady enlightenment. He who is enlightened to the Truth achieves liberation from bondage, and he who is truly liberated experiences eternal joy.

376 I know of no higher source of happiness for a self-controlled man than dispassion, and when allied to thoroughly pure self-knowledge it leads to the sovereign state of self-mastery. Since this is the gate to the unfading maiden of liberation, always and with all eagerness develop this supreme wisdom within yourself in happiness.

āśāṃ chinddhi viṣopameṣu viṣayeṣveṣaiva mṛtyoḥ kṛtis
tyaktvā jātikulāśrameṣvabhimatiṃ muñcātidūrātkriyāḥ |
dehādāvasati tyajātmadhiṣaṇāṃ prajñāṃ kuruṣvātmani
tvaṃ draṣṭāsyamano'si nirdvayaparaṃ brahmāsi yadvastutaḥ || 377 ||

lakṣye brahmaṇi mānasaṃ dṛḍhataraṃ saṃsthāpya bāhyendriyaṃ
svasthāne viniveśya niścalatanuścopekṣya dehasthitim |
brahmātmaikyamupetya tanmāyātayā cākhaṇḍavṛttyāniśaṃ
brahmānandarasaṃ pibātmani mudā śūnyaiḥ kimanyairbhṛśam || 378 ||

anātmacintanaṃ tyaktvā kaśmalaṃ duḥkhakāraṇam |
cintayātmānamānandarūpaṃ yanmuktikāraṇam || 379 ||

eṣa svayaṃjyotiraśeṣasākṣī
vijñānakośo vilasatyajasram |
lakṣyaṃ vidhāyainamasadvilakṣaṇam
akhaṇḍavṛttyātmatayānubhāvaya || 380 ||

etamacchinnayā vṛttyā pratyayāntaraśūnyayā |
ullekhayanvijānīyātsvasvarūpatayā sphuṭam || 381 ||

atrātmatvaṃ dṛḍhīkurvannahamādiṣu saṃtyajan |
udāsīnatayā teṣu tiṣṭhetsphuṭaghaṭādivat || 382 ||

viśuddhamantaḥkaraṇaṃ svarūpe
niveśya sākṣiṇyavabodhamātre |
śanaiḥ śanairniścalatāmupānayan
pūrṇaṃ svamevānuvilokayettataḥ || 383 ||

dehendriyaprāṇamano'hamādibhiḥ
svājñānakḷptairakhilairupādhibhiḥ |
vimuktamātmānamakhaṇḍarūpaṃ
pūrṇaṃ mahākāśamivāvalokayet || 384 ||

377 Cut off desire for the poison-like senses, for these are death-dealing. Get rid of pride in birth, family and state of life, and throw achievements far away. Drop such unreal things as the body into the sacrificial bowl of your true self, and develop wisdom within. You are the Witness. You are beyond the thinking mind. You are truly God, non-dual and supreme.

378 Direct the mind resolutely towards God, restraining the senses in their various seats, and looking on the state of the body as a matter of indifference. Realize your oneness with God, remaining continually intent on identifying with its nature, and joyfully drink the bliss of God within, for what use is there in other, empty things?

379 Stop thinking about anything which is not your true self, for that is degrading and productive of pain, and instead think about your true nature, which is bliss itself and productive of liberation.

380 This treasure of consciousness shines unfading with its own light as the witness of everything. Meditate continually on it, making this your aim, distinct as it is from the unreal.

381 This one should be aware of with unbroken application, continually turning to it with a mind empty of everything else, knowing it to be one's own true nature.

382 This one should identify with firmly, abandoning the sense of doership and so on, remaining indifferent to them, as one is to things like a cracked jar.

383 Turning one's purified awareness within on the witness as pure consciousness, one should gradually bring it to stillness and then become aware of the perfection of one's true nature.

384 One should become aware of oneself, indivisible and perfect like Space itself, when free from identification with such things as one's body, senses, functions, mind and sense of doership, which are all the products of one's own ignorance.

ghaṭakalaśakusūlasūcimukhyaiḥ
gaganamupādhiśatairvimuktamekam |
bhavati na vividhaṃ tathaiva śuddhaṃ
paramahamādivimuktamekameva || 385 ||

brahmādistambaparyantā mṛṣāmātrā upādhayaḥ |
tataḥ pūrṇaṃ svamātmānaṃ paśyedekātmanā sthitam || 386 ||

yatra bhrāntyā kalpitaṃ tadviveke
tattanmātraṃ naiva tasmādvibhinnam |
bhrānternāśe bhāti dṛṣṭāhitattvaṃ
rajjustadvadviśvamātmasvarūpam || 387 ||

svayaṃ brahmā svayaṃ viṣṇuḥ svayamindraḥ svayaṃ śivaḥ |
svayaṃ viśvamidaṃ sarvaṃ svasmādanyanna kiṃcana || 388 ||

antaḥ svayaṃ cāpi bahiḥ svayaṃ ca
svayaṃ purastātsvayameva paścāt |
svayaṃ hyāvācyāṃ svayamapyudīcyāṃ
tathopariṣṭātsvayamapyadhastāt || 389 ||

taraṅgaphenabhramabudbudādi
sarvaṃ svarūpeṇa jalaṃ yathā tathā |
cideva dehādyahamantametat
sarvaṃ cidevaikarasaṃ viśuddham || 390 ||

sadevedaṃ sarvaṃ jagadavagataṃ vāṅmanasayoḥ
sato'nyannāstyeva prakṛtiparasīmni sthitavataḥ |
pṛthakkiṃ mṛtsnāyāḥ kalaśaghaṭakumbhādyavagataṃ
vadatyeṣa bhrāntastvamahamiti māyāmadirayā || 391 ||

kriyāsamabhihāreṇa yatra nānyaditi śrutiḥ |
bravīti dvaitarāhityaṃ mithyādhyāsanivṛttaye || 392 ||

385 Space when freed from the hundreds of additional objects like pots and pans, receptacles and needles is one, and in the same way the supreme Reality becomes no longer multiple but one and pure when freed from the sense of doership and so on.

386 All additional objects from Brahma to the last clump of grass are simply unreal, so one should be aware of one's own perfect true nature abiding alone and by itself.

387 When rightly seen, what had been mistaken in error for something else is only what it always was and not something different. When the mistaken perception is removed the reality of the rope is seen for what it is, and the same is true for the way everything is really oneself.

388 One is oneself Brahma, one is Vishnu, one is Indra, one is Shiva, and one is oneself all this. Nothing else exists except oneself.

389 Oneself is what is within, oneself is without, oneself is in front and oneself is behind. Oneself is to the south, oneself is to the north, and oneself is also above and below.

390 Just as waves, foam, whirlpool and bubbles are all in reality just water, so consciousness is all this from the body to the sense of doership. Everything is just the one pure consciousness.

391 This whole world known to speech and mind is really the supreme Reality. Nothing else exists but the Reality situated beyond the limits of the natural world. Are pots, jars, tubs and so on different from clay? It is the man confused by the wine of Māyā that talks of "you" and "me".

392 The scripture talks of the absence of duality in the expression "where there is nothing else"[31] with several verbs to remove any idea of false attribution.

31 Chandogya Upanishad 7.24.1.

ākāśavannirmalanirvikalpaṃ
niḥsīmaniḥspandananirvikāram |
antarbahiḥśūnyamananyamadvayaṃ
svayaṃ paraṃ brahma kimasti bodhyam || 393 ||

vaktavyaṃ kimu vidyate'tra bahudhā brahmaiva jīvaḥ svayaṃ
brahmaitajjagadātataṃ nu sakalaṃ brahmādvitīyaṃ śrutiḥ |
brahmaivāhamiti prabuddhamatayaḥ saṃtyaktabāhyāḥ sphuṭaṃ
brahmībhūya vasanti santatacidānandātmanaitaddhruvam || 394 ||

jahi malamāyākośe'haṃdhiyotthāpitāśāṃ
prasabhamanilakalpe liṅgadehe'pi paścāt |
nigamagaditakīrtiṃ nityamānandamūrtiṃ
svayamiti paricīya brahmarūpeṇa tiṣṭha || 395 ||

śavākāraṃ yāvadbhajati manujastāvadaśuciḥ
parebhyaḥ syātkleśo jananamaraṇavyādhinilayaḥ |
yadātmānaṃ śuddhaṃ kalayati śivākāramacalam
tadā tebhyo mukto bhavati hi tadāha śrutirapi || 396 ||

svātmanyāropitāśeṣābhāsarvastunirāsataḥ |
svayameva paraṃ brahma pūrṇamadvayamakriyam || 397 ||

samāhitāyāṃ sati cittavṛttau
parātmani brahmaṇi nirvikalpe |
na dṛśyate kaścidayaṃ vikalpaḥ
prajalpamātraḥ pariśiṣyate yataḥ || 398 ||

asatkalpo vikalpo'yaṃ viśvamityekavastuni |
nirvikāre nirākāre nirviśeṣe bhidā kutaḥ || 399 ||

draṣṭudarśanadṛśyādibhāvaśūnyaikavastuni |
nirvikāre nirākāre nirviśeṣe bhidā kutaḥ || 400 ||

kalpārṇava ivātyantaparipūrṇaikavastuni |
nirvikāre nirākāre nirviśeṣe bhidā kutaḥ || 401 ||

393 What else is there to know but one's true supreme nature, God himself, like space pure, imageless, unmoving, unchanging, free of within or without, without a second and non-dual.

394 What more is to be said here? The individual is himself God. Scripture declares that this whole extended world is the indivisible God. Those who have been illuminated by the thought "I am God", themselves live steadfastly as God, abandoning external objects, as the eternal consciousness and bliss.

395 Destroy the desires arising from opinions about yourself in this impure body, and even more so those of the subtle mental level, and remain as yourself, the God within, the eternal body of bliss, celebrated by the scriptures.

396 So long as a man is concerned about the corpse-like body, he is impure and suffers from his enemies in the shape of birth, death and sickness. When however he thinks of himself as pure godlike and immovable, then he is freed from those enemies, as the scriptures proclaim.

397 Getting rid of all apparent realities within oneself, one is oneself the supreme God, perfect, non-dual and actionless.

398 When the mind waves are put to rest in one's true nature, the imageless God, then this false assumption exists no longer, but is recognized as just empty talk.

399 What we call "All this" is a false idea and mistaken assumption of in the one Reality. How can there be distinctions in something which is changeless, formless and without characteristics?

400 Seer, seeing and seen and so on have no existence in the one Reality. How can there be distinctions in something which is changeless, formless and without characteristics?

401 In the one Reality which is completely perfect like the primal ocean, how can there be distinctions in something which is changeless, formless and without characteristics?

tejasīva tamo yatra pralīnaṃ bhrāntikāraṇam |
advitīye pare tattve nirviśeṣe bhidā kutaḥ || 402 ||

ekātmake pare tattve bhedavārtā kathaṃ vaset |
suṣuptau sukhamātrāyāṃ bhedaḥ kenāvalokitaḥ || 403 ||

na hyasti viśvaṃ paratattvabodhāt
sadātmani brahmaṇi nirvikalpe |
kālatraye nāpyahirīkṣito guṇe
na hyambubindurmṛgatṛṣṇikāyām || 404 ||

māyāmātramidaṃ dvaitamadvaitaṃ paramārthataḥ |
iti brūte śrutiḥ sākṣātsuṣuptāvanubhūyate || 405 ||

ananyatvamadhiṣṭhānādāropyasya nirīkṣitam |
paṇḍitai rajjusarpādau vikalpo bhrāntijīvanaḥ || 406 ||

cittamūlo vikalpo'yaṃ cittābhāve na kaścana |
ataścittaṃ samādhehi pratyagrūpe parātmani || 407 ||

kimapi satatabodhaṃ kevalānandarūpaṃ
nirupamamativelaṃ nityamuktaṃ nirīham |
niravadhigaganābhaṃ niṣkalaṃ nirvikalpaṃ
hṛdi kalayati vidvān brahma pūrṇaṃ samādhau || 408 ||

prakṛtivikṛtiśūnyaṃ bhāvanātītabhāvaṃ
samarasamasamānaṃ mānasaṃ bandhadūram |
nigamavacanasiddhaṃ nityamasmatprasiddhaṃ
hṛdi kalayati vidvān brahma pūrṇaṃ samādhau || 409 ||

ajaramamaramastābhāvavastusvarūpaṃ
stimitasalilarāśiprakhyamākhyāvihīnam |
śamitaguṇavikāraṃ śāśvataṃ śāntamekaṃ
hṛdi kalayati vidvān brahma pūrṇaṃ samādhau || 410 ||

402 When the cause of error has been annihilated like darkness in light, how can there be distinctions in something which is changeless, formless and without characteristics?

403 How can there be distinctions in a supreme reality which is by nature one? Who has noticed any distinctions in the pure joy of deep sleep?

404 After realization of the supreme Truth, all this no longer exists in one's true nature of the imageless God. The snake is not to be found in time past, present or future, and not a drop of water is to be found in a mirage.

405 Scripture declares that this dualism is Māyā-created and actually non-dual in the final analysis. It is experienced for oneself in deep sleep.

406 The identity of a projection with its underlying reality is recognized by the wise in the case of the rope and the snake, etc. The false assumption arises from a mistake.

407 This falsely imagined reality depends on thought, and in the absence of thought it no longer exists, so put thought to rest in samadhi in the inner reality of one's higher nature.

408 The wise man experiences the perfection of God in his heart in samadhi as something which is eternal consciousness, complete bliss, incomparable, transcendent, ever free, free from effort, and like infinite space indivisible and unimaginable.

409 The wise man experiences the perfection of God in his heart in samadhi as something which is free from natural causation, a reality beyond thought, uniform, unequalled, far from the associations of pride, vouched for by the pronouncements of scripture, eternal, and familiar to us as ourselves.

410 The wise man experiences the perfection of God in his heart in samadhi as something which is unaging, undying, the abiding reality among changing objects, formless, like a calm sea free from questions and answers, where the effects of natural attributes are at rest, eternal, peaceful and one.

samāhitāntaḥkaraṇaḥ svarūpe
vilokayātmānamakhaṇḍavaibhavam |
vicchinddhi bandhaṃ bhavagandhagandhitaṃ
yatnena puṃstvaṃ saphalīkuruṣva || 411 ||

sarvopādhivinirmuktaṃ saccidānandamadvayam |
bhāvayātmānamātmasthaṃ na bhūyaḥ kalpase'dhvane || 412 ||

chāyeva puṃsaḥ paridṛśyamān
mābhāsarūpeṇa phalānubhūtyā |
śarīramārācchavavannirastaṃ
punarna saṃdhatta idaṃ mahātmā || 413 ||

satatavimalabodhānandarūpaṃ sametya
tyaja jaḍamalarūpopādhimetaṃ sudūre |
atha punarapi naiṣa smaryatāṃ vāntavastu
smaraṇaviṣayabhūtaṃ palpate kutsanāya || 414 ||

samūlametatparidāhya vanhau
sadātmani brahmaṇi nirvikalpe |
tataḥ svayaṃ nityaviśuddhabodhā
nandātmanā tiṣṭhati vidvariṣṭhaḥ || 415 ||

prārabdhasūtragrathitaṃ śarīraṃ
prayātu vā tiṣṭhatu goriva srak |
na tatpunaḥ paśyati tattvavettā
(ā)nandātmani brahmaṇi līnavṛttiḥ || 416 ||

akhaṇḍānandamātmānaṃ vijñāya svasvarūpataḥ |
kimicchan kasya vā hetordehaṃ puṣṇāti tattvavit || 417 ||

saṃsiddhasya phalaṃ tvetajjīvanmuktasya yoginaḥ |
bahirantaḥ sadānandarasāsvādanamātmani || 418 ||

vairāgyasya phalaṃ bodho bodhasyoparatiḥ phalam |
svānandānubhavācchāntireṣaivoparateḥ phalam || 419 ||

411 With the mind pacified by samadhi within, recognize the infinite glory of yourself, sever the sweet-smelling bonds of samsara, and energetically become one who has achieved the goal of human existence.

412 Free from all false self-identification, meditate on yourself as the non-dual being-consciousness-bliss within yourself, and you will no longer be subject to samsara.

413 Seeing it as no more than a man's shadow, a mere reflection brought about by causality, the sage looks on his body as from a distance like a corpse, with no intention of taking it up again.

414 Come to the eternally pure reality of consciousness and bliss and reject afar identification with this dull and unclean body. Don't remember it any more, like something once vomited is fit only for contempt.

415 Burning this down along with its roots in the fire of his true nature, the imageless God, the wise man remains alone in his nature as eternally pure consciousness and bliss.

416 Let the body, spun on the thread of previous causation, fall or stay put, like a cows garland. The knower of the Truth takes no more notice of it, as his mental functions are merged in his true nature of God.

417 To satisfy what desire, or for what purpose should the knower of the Truth care for his body, when he knows himself in his own true nature of indivisible bliss.

418 The fruit gained by the successful man, liberated here and now, is the enjoyment in himself of the experience of being and bliss within and without.

419 The fruit of dispassion is understanding, the fruit of understanding is imperturbability, and the fruit of the experience of bliss within is peace. This is the fruit of imperturbability.

yadyuttarottarābhāvaḥ pūrvapūrvantu niṣphalam |
nivṛttiḥ paramā tṛptirānando'nupamaḥ svataḥ || 420 ||

dṛṣṭaduḥkheṣvanudvego vidyāyāḥ prastutaṃ phalam |
yatkṛtaṃ bhrāntivelāyāṃ nānā karma jugupsitam
paścānnaro vivekena tatkathaṃ kartumarhati || 421 ||

vidyāphalaṃ syādasato nivṛttiḥ
pravṛttirajñānaphalaṃ tadīkṣitam |
tajjñājñayoryanmṛgatṛṣṇikādau
nocedvidāṃ dṛṣṭaphalaṃ kimasmāt || 422 ||

ajñānahṛdayagranthervināśo yadyaśeṣataḥ |
anicchorviṣayaḥ kiṃ nu pravṛtteḥ kāraṇaṃ svataḥ || 423 ||

vāsanānudayo bhogye vairāgasya tadāvadhiḥ |
ahaṃbhāvodayābhāvo bodhasya paramāvadhiḥ
līnavṛttairanutpattirmaryādoparatestu sā || 424 ||

brahmākāratayā sadā sthitatayā nirmuktabāhyārthadhīr
anyāveditabhogyabhogakalano nidrāluvadbālavat |
svapnālokitalokavajjagadidaṃ paśyan kvacillabdhadhīr
āste kaścidanantapuṇyaphalabhugdhanyaḥ sa mānyo bhuvi || 425 ||

sthitaprajño yatirayaṃ yaḥ sadānandamaśnute |
brahmaṇyeva vilīnātmā nirvikāro viniṣkriyaḥ || 426 ||

brahmātmanoḥ śodhitayorekabhāvāvagāhinī |
nirvikalpā ca cinmātrā vṛttiḥ prajñeti kathyate
susthitāsau bhavedyasya sthitaprajñaḥ sa ucyate || 427 ||

420 If the successive stages do not occur it means that the previous ones were ineffective. Tranquillity is the supreme satisfaction, leading to incomparable bliss.

421 The fruit of insight referred to is feeling no disquiet at the experience of suffering. How could a man who has done various disgusting actions in a time of aberration do the same again when he is in his right mind?

422 The fruit of knowledge should be the turning away from the unreal, while turning towards the unreal is seen to be the fruit of ignorance. This can be seen in the case of some-one who recognizes or does not recognize things like a mirage. Otherwise what fruit would there be for seers?

423 When the knot of the heart, ignorance, has been thoroughly removed, how could the senses be the cause of the mind being directed outwards for some-one who does not want them?

424 When there is no upsurge of desire for goods, that is the summit of dispassion. When there is no longer any occurrence of the self-identification with the doer, that is the summit of understanding, and when there is no more arising of latent mental activity, that is the summit of equanimity.

425 He is the enjoyer of the fruit of infinite past good deeds, blessed and to be revered on earth, who free from external things by always been established in his awareness of God, regards objects which others look on as desirable like some-one half asleep, or like a child, and who looks at the world like a world seen in a dream, or like some mere chance encounter.

426 That ascetic is of established wisdom who enjoys the experience of being and bliss with his mind merged in God, beyond change and beyond action.

427 That function of the mind which is imageless pure awareness, and which is immersed in the essential oneness of oneself and God is known as wisdom, and he in whom this state is well established is called one of established wisdom.

yasya sthitā bhavetprajñā yasyānando nirantaraḥ |
prapañco vismṛtaprāyaḥ sa jīvanmukta iṣyate || 428 ||

līnadhīrapi jāgarti jāgraddharmavivarjitaḥ |
bodho nirvāsano yasya sa jīvanmukta iṣyate || 429 ||

śāntasaṃsārakalanaḥ kalāvānapi niṣkalaḥ |
yasya cittaṃ viniścintaṃ sa jīvanmukta iṣyate || 430 ||

vartamāne'pi dehe'smiñchāyāvadanuvartini |
ahantāmamatābhāvo jīvanmuktasya lakṣaṇam || 431 ||

atītānanusandhānaṃ bhaviṣyadavicāraṇam |
audāsīnyamapi prāptaṃ jīvanmuktasya lakṣaṇam || 432 ||

guṇadoṣaviśiṣṭe'sminsvabhāvena vilakṣaṇe |
sarvatra samadarśitvaṃ jīvanmuktasya lakṣaṇam || 433 ||

iṣṭāniṣṭārthasamprāptau samadarśitayātmani |
ubhayatrāvikāritvaṃ jīvanmuktasya lakṣaṇam || 434 ||

brahmānandarasāsvādāsaktacittatayā yateḥ |
antarbahiravijñānaṃ jīvanmuktasya lakṣaṇam || 435 ||

dehendriyādau kartavye mamāhaṃbhāvavarjitaḥ |
audāsīnyena yastiṣṭhetsa jīvanmuktalakṣaṇaḥ || 436 ||

vijñāta ātmano yasya brahmabhāvaḥ śruterbalāt |
bhavabandhavinirmuktaḥ sa jīvanmuktalakṣaṇaḥ || 437 ||

428 He whose wisdom is well established, whose bliss is uninterrupted, and whose awareness of multiplicity is virtually forgotten, he is regarded as liberated here and now.

429 When a man's mind is at rest in God even when he is awake he does not share the usual condition of being awake. He whose awareness is free of desires is regarded as liberated here and now.

430 He whose worries in samsara have been put to rest, who though made up of parts does not identify himself with them, and whose mind is free from thoughts, he is regarded as liberated here and now.

431 The sign of a man liberated here and now is the absence of thoughts of "me" and "mine" in the body while it still exists, going along with him like his shadow.

432 The sign of a man liberated here and now is not running back to the past, not dwelling on the future, and being unconcerned about the present.

433 The sign of a man liberated here and now is to look with an equal eye on everything in this manifold existence with all its natural faults, knowing that in itself it is without characteristics.

434 The sign of a man liberated here and now is to remain unmoved in either direction, looking on things with an equal eye within, whether encountering the pleasant or the painful.

435 The sign of a man liberated here and now is to be unaware of internal or external, since the ascetic's mind is occupied with enjoying the experience of the bliss of God.

436 The sign of a man liberated here and now is that he remains unconcerned and free from the sense of "me" and "mine" in the things needing to be done by the body and the senses and so on.

437 The sign of a man liberated here and now is that he is free from the bonds of samsara, knowing his own identity with God with the help of the scriptures.

dehendriyeṣvahaṃbhāva idaṃbhāvastadanyake |
yasya no bhavataḥ kvāpi sa jīvanmukta iṣyate || 438 ||

na pratyagbrahmaṇorbhedaṃ kadāpi brahmasargayoḥ |
prajñayā yo vijāniti sa jīvanmuktalakṣaṇaḥ || 439 ||

sādhubhiḥ pūjyamāne'smin pīḍyamāne'pi durjanaiḥ |
samabhāvo bhavedyasya sa jīvanmuktalakṣaṇaḥ || 440 ||

yatra praviṣṭā viṣayāḥ pareritā
nadīpravāhā iva vārirāśau |
linanti sanmātratayā na vikriyāṃ
utpādayantyeṣa yatirvimuktaḥ || 441 ||

vijñātabrahmatattvasya yathāpūrvaṃ na saṃsṛtiḥ |
asti cenna sa vijñātabrahmabhāvo bahirmukhaḥ || 442 ||

prācīnavāsanāvegādasau saṃsaratīti cet |
na sadekatvavijñānānmandī bhavati vāsanā || 443 ||

atyantakāmukasyāpi vṛttiḥ kuṇṭhati mātari |
tathaiva brahmaṇi jñāte pūrṇānande manīṣiṇaḥ || 444 ||

nididhyāsanaśīlasya bāhyapratyaya īkṣyate |
bravīti śrutiretasya prārabdhaṃ phaladarśanāt || 445 ||

sukhādyanubhavo yāvattāvatprārabdhamiṣyate |
phalodayaḥ kriyāpūrvo niṣkriyo na hi kutracit || 446 ||

ahaṃ brahmeti vijñānātkalpakoṭiśatārjitam |
sañcitaṃ vilayaṃ yāti prabodhātsvapnakarmavat || 447 ||

yatkṛtaṃ svapnavelāyāṃ puṇyaṃ vā pāpamulbaṇam |
suptotthitasya kiṃ tatsyātsvargāya narakāya vā || 448 ||

438 He is regarded as liberated here and now who has no sense of "this is me" in the body and senses, nor of "it exists" in anything else.

439 The sign of a man liberated here and now is that he knows by wisdom that there is never any distinction between God and what proceeds from God.

440 The sign of a man liberated here and now is that he remains the same whether he is revered by the good or tortured by the bad.

441 That ascetic is liberated into whom, because of his being pure reality, the sense object can flow and merge without leaving any alteration, like the water of a river's flow.

442 There is no more samsara for him who knows the Truth of God as there was before. If there is, then it is not the knowledge of God, since it is still outward turned.

443 If it is suggested that he still experiences samsara because of the strength of his previous desires, the answer is, No, desires become powerless through the knowledge of one's oneness with Reality.

444 The impulses of even an extremely passionate man are arrested in face of his mother, and in the same way those of the wise cease in face of the perfect bliss of the knowledge of God.

445 Some-one practising meditation is seen to have external functions still. Scripture declares that this is the effect of the fruits of previous conditioning.

446 So long as pleasure and the like occur, one acknowledges the effect of previous conditioning. A result occurs because of a previous cause. Nothing happens without a cause.

447 With the realization that "I am God", all the actions accumulated over ages are wiped out, like actions in a dream on waking up.

448 How could the good or even dreadfully bad deeds done in the dreaming state lead a man to heaven or hell when he arises from sleep?

svamasaṅgamudāsīnaṃ parijñāya nabho yathā |
na śliṣyati ca yatkiṃcitkadācidbhāvikarmabhiḥ || 449 ||

na nabho ghaṭayogena surāgandhena lipyate |
tathātmopādhiyogena taddharmairnaiva lipyate || 450 ||

jñānodayātpurārabdhaṃ karmajñānānna naśyati |
adatvā svaphalaṃ lakṣyamuddiśyotsṛṣṭabāṇavat || 451 ||

vyāghrabuddhyā vinirmukto bāṇaḥ paścāttu gomatau |
na tiṣṭhati chinatyeva lakṣyaṃ vegena nirbharam || 452 ||

prābdhaṃ balavattaraṃ khalu vidāṃ bhogena tasya kṣayaḥ
samyagjñānahutāśanena vilayaḥ prākṣaṃcitāgāminām |
brahmātmaikyamavekṣya tanmāyātayā ye sarvadā saṃsthitāḥ
teṣāṃ tattritayaṃ nahi kvacidapi brahmaiva te nirguṇam || 453 ||

upādhitādātmyavihīnakevala
brahmātmanaivātmani tiṣṭhato muneḥ |
prārabdhasadbhāvakathā na yuktā
svapnārthasaṃbandhakatheva jāgrataḥ || 454 ||

na hi prabuddhaḥ pratibhāsadehe
dehopayoginyapi ca prapañce |
karotyahantāṃ mamatānidantāṃ
kintu svayaṃ tiṣṭhati jāgareṇa || 455 ||

na tasya mithyārthasamarthanecchā
na saṃgrahastajjagato'pi dṛṣṭaḥ |
tatrānuvṛttiryadi cenmṛṣārthe
na nidrayā mukta itīṣyate dhruvam || 456 ||

449 Recognizing himself as unattached and impartial space, he never hold on to anything with the thought of actions yet to be done.

450 Space is not affected with the smell of wine by contact with the jar, and in the same way one's true nature is not affected by their qualities through contact with the things one identified oneself with.

451 The karma created before the arising of knowledge does not come to an end with knowledge without producing its effect, like an arrow shot at a target after being loosed.

452 An arrow released in the understanding that it was at a tiger does not stop when it is seen to be a cow, but pierces the target with the full force of its speed.

453 The effects of previous conditioning are too strong for even a wise man, and it is eliminated only by enduring it, but the effects of present and future conditioning are all destroyed by the fire of true understanding. Those who are always established in the knowledge of their oneness with God, as a result of that are not affected by these three aspects of conditioning since they share the unconditioned nature of God.

454 The question of the existence of past conditioning does not apply for the ascetic who, by getting rid of self-identification with anything else, is established within in the knowledge of the perfection of God as his true nature, just as questions concerned with things in a dream have no meaning when one has woken up.

455 He who has woken up makes no distinctions about his dream body and the multiplicity of things connected with it as being "me", "mine" or anything else, but simply remains himself by staying awake.

456 He has no desire to assert the reality of those illusions, and he has no need to hold on to the things he has woken up from. If he still chases these false realities he is certainly considered not awake yet.

tadvatpare brahmaṇi vartamānaḥ
sadātmanā tiṣṭhati nānyadīkṣate |
smṛtiryathā svapnavilokitārthe
tathā vidaḥ prāśanamocanādau || 457 ||

karmaṇā nirmito dehaḥ prārabdhaṃ tasya kalpyatām |
nānāderātmano yuktaṃ naivātmā karmanirmitaḥ || 458 ||

ajo nityaḥ śāśvata iti brūte śrutiramoghavāk |
tadātmanā tiṣṭhato'sya kutaḥ prārabdhakalpanā || 459 ||

prārabdhaṃ sidhyati tadā yadā dehātmanā sthitiḥ |
dehātmabhāvo naiveṣṭaḥ prārabdhaṃ tyajyatāmataḥ || 460 ||

śarīrasyāpi prārabdhakalpanā bhrāntireva hi |
adhyastasya kutaḥ sattvamasatyasya kuto janiḥ
ajātasya kuto nāśaḥ prārabdhamasataḥ kutaḥ || 461 ||

jñānenājñānakāryasya samūlasya layo yadi |
tiṣṭhatyayaṃ kathaṃ deha iti śaṅkāvato jaḍān || 462 ||
samādhātuṃ bāhyadṛṣṭyā prārabdhaṃ vadati śrutiḥ |
na tu dehādisatyatvabodhanāya vipaścitām || 463 ||

paripūrṇamanādyantamaprameyamavikriyam |
ekamevādvayaṃ brahma neha nānāsti kiṃcana || 464 ||

sadganaṃ cidghanaṃ nityamānandaghanamakriyam |
ekamevādvayaṃ brahma neha nānāsti kiṃcana || 465 ||

pratyagekarasaṃ pūrṇamanantaṃ sarvatomukham |
ekamevādvayaṃ brahma neha nānāsti kiṃcana || 466 ||

457 In the same way he who lives in God remains in his own nature and seeks nothing else. Like the memory of things seen in a dream is the way the seer experiences eating, going to the toilet and so on.

458 The body has been formed by causation so past causality appropriately applies to it, but it does not apply to the beginningless self, since one's true nature has not been causally formed.

459 Scriptures which do not err affirm that one's true nature is "Unborn, eternal and abiding",[32] so how could causality apply to someone established in such a self?

460 Causality applies only so long as one identifies oneself with the body, so he who does not consider himself the body has abolished causality for himself.

461 Even the opinion that causality applies to the body is a mistake. How can a false assumption be true, and how can something which does not exist have a beginning? How can something with no beginning have an end, and how can causality apply to something that does not exist?

462–63 The ignorant have the problem that if ignorance has been completely eliminated by knowledge, how does the body persist? To settle this doubt scripture talks about causality in accordance with conventional views, but not to teach the reality of the body and such things to the wise.

464 Complete in himself, without beginning or end, infinite and unchanging, God is one and without a second. There is nothing other than He.

465 The essence of Truth, the essence of Consciousness, the eternal essence of Bliss and unchanging, God is one and without a second. There is nothing other than He.

466 The one reality within everything, complete, infinite, and limitless, God is one and without a second. There is nothing other than He.

32 Katha Upanishad 1.2.18.

aheyamanupādeyamanādeyamanāśrayam |
ekamevādvayaṃ brahma neha nānāsti kiṃcana || 467 ||

nirguṇaṃ niṣkalaṃ sūkṣmaṃ nirvikalpaṃ nirañjanam |
ekamevādvayaṃ brahma neha nānāsti kiṃcana || 468 ||

anirūpya svarūpaṃ yanmanovācāmagocaram |
ekamevādvayaṃ brahma neha nānāsti kiṃcana || 469 ||

satsamṛddhaṃ svataḥsiddhaṃ śuddhaṃ buddhamanīdṛśam |
ekamevādvayaṃ brahma neha nānāsti kiṃcana || 470 ||

nirastarāgā vinirastabhogāḥ
śāntāḥ sudāntā yatayo mahāntaḥ |
vijñāya tattvaṃ parametadante
prāptāḥ parāṃ nirvṛtimātmayogāt || 471 ||

bhavānapīdaṃ paratattvamātmanaḥ
svarūpamānandaghanaṃ vicārya |
vidhūya mohaṃ svamanaḥprakalpitaṃ
muktaḥ kṛtārtho bhavatu prabuddhaḥ || 472 ||

samādhinā sādhuviniścalātmanā
paśyātmatattvaṃ sphuṭabodhacakṣuṣā |
niḥsaṃśayaṃ samyagavekṣitaścec
chrutaḥ padārtho na punarvikalpyate || 473 ||

svasyāvidyābandhasaṃbandhamokṣāt
satyajñānānandarūpātmalabdhau |
śāstraṃ yuktirdeśikoktiḥ pramāṇaṃ
cāntaḥsiddhā svānubhūtiḥ pramāṇam || 474 ||

bandho mokṣaśca tṛptiśca cintārogyakṣudādayaḥ |
svenaiva vedyā yajjñānaṃ pareṣāmānumānikam || 475 ||

taṭasthitā bodhayanti guravaḥ śrutayo yathā |
prajñayaiva taredvidvānīśvarānugṛhītayā || 476 ||

467 He cannot be removed or grasped; he cannot be received from someone else, or held onto. God is one and without a second. There is nothing other than He.

468 Without attributes, indivisible, subtle, inconceivable, and without blemish, God is one and without a second. There is nothing other than He.

469 His appearance is formless, beyond the realm of mind and speech. God is one and without a second. There is nothing other than He.

470 Exuberant Reality, self-reliant, complete, pure, conscious and unique, God is one and without a second. There is nothing other than He.

471 Great ascetics who have abandoned desires and given up possessions, calm and disciplined, come to know this supreme Truth, and in the end attain the supreme peace by their self-realization.

472 You too should recognize this supreme Truth about yourself, your true nature and the essence of bliss, and shaking off the illusion created by your own imagination, become liberated, fulfilled and enlightened.

473 See the Truth of yourself with the clear eye of understanding, after the mind has been made thoroughly unwavering by meditation. If the words of scripture you have heard are really received without doubting, you will experience no more mistaken perception.

474 When one has freed oneself from association with the bonds of ignorance by the realization of the reality of Truth, Wisdom and Bliss, then scripture, traditional practices and the sayings of the wise remain proofs, but the inner experience of truth is proof too.

475 Bondage, freedom, contentment, worry, health, hunger and so on are matters of personal experience, and other people's knowledge of them can only be by inference.

476 Impartial gurus teach, as do the scriptures, that the wise man crosses over by means of wisdom alone through the grace of God.

svānubhūtyā svayaṃ jñātvā svamātmānamakhaṇḍitam |
saṃsiddhaḥ saṃmukhaṃ tiṣṭhennirvikalpātmanātmani || 477 ||

vedāntasiddhāntaniruktireṣā
brahmaiva jīvaḥ sakalaṃ jagacca |
akhaṇḍarūpasthitireva mokṣo
brahmādvitīye śrutayaḥ pramāṇam || 478 ||

iti guruvacanācchrutipramāṇāt
paramavagamya satattvamātmayuktyā |
praśamitakaraṇaḥ samāhitātmā
kvacidacalākṛtirātmaniṣṭhato'bhūt || 479 ||

kiṃcitkālaṃ samādhāya pare brahmaṇi mānasam |
utthāya paramānandādidaṃ vacanamabravīt || 480 ||

buddhirvinaṣṭā galitā pravṛttiḥ
brahmātmanorekatayādhigatyā |
idaṃ na jāne'pyanidaṃ na jāne
kiṃ vā kiyadvā sukhamastyapāram || 481 ||

vācā vaktumaśakyameva manasā mantuṃ na vā śakyate
svānandāmṛtapūrapūritaparabrahmāmbudhervaibhavam |
ambhorāśiviśīrṇavārṣikaśilābhāvaṃ bhajanme mano
yasyāṃśāṃśalave vilīnamadhunānandātmanā nirvṛtam || 482 ||

kva gataṃ kena vā nītaṃ kutra līnamidaṃ jagat |
adhunaiva mayā dṛṣṭaṃ nāsti kiṃ mahadadbhutam || 483 ||

kiṃ heyaṃ kimupādeyaṃ kimanyatkiṃ vilakṣaṇam |
akhaṇḍānandapīyūṣapūrṇe brahmamahārṇave || 484 ||

na kiṃcidatra paśyāmi na śṛṇomi na vedmyaham |
svātmanaiva sadānandarūpeṇāsmi vilakṣaṇaḥ || 485 ||

477 Knowing his true indivisible nature by his own realization the perfected man should remain in full possession of himself free from imaginations within.

478 The conclusion of all the scriptures and of experience is that God is the individual and the whole world too, and that liberation is to remain in the one indivisible Reality. The scriptures are also the authority for the non-duality of God.

479 Having thus attained the supreme reality by self discipline through the words of his guru and the testimony of the scriptures, his faculties at peace and his mind at peace, he becomes something self-poised and immovable.

480 Having established his mind for some time in the supreme God, he arose from supreme bliss and uttered these words.

481 My intellect has vanished and my mental activities have been swallowed up in the realization of the oneness of myself and God. I no longer know this from that, nor what or how great this unsurpassed joy is.

482 Words cannot express nor the mind conceive the greatness of the ocean of the supreme God, full of the nectar of bliss. Like the state of a hail-stone fallen into the ocean, my mind has now melted away in the tiniest fraction of it, fulfilled by its essential nature of Bliss.

483 Where has the world gone? Who has removed it, or where has it disappeared to? I saw it only just now, and now it is not there. This a great wonder.

484 In the great ocean filled with the nectar of the indivisible bliss of God, what is to be got rid of, what is to be held onto, what is there apart from oneself and what has any characteristics of its own?

485 I can neither see, hear or experience anything else there, as it is I who exist there by myself with the characteristics of Being and Bliss.

namo namaste gurave mahātmane
vimuktasaṅgāya saduttamāya |
nityādvayānandarasasvarūpiṇe
bhūmne sadāpāradayāmbudhāmne || 486 ||

yatkaṭākṣaśaśisāndracandrikā
pātadhūtabhavatāpajaśramaḥ |
prāptavānahamakhaṇḍavaibhavā
nandamātmapadamakṣayaṃ kṣaṇāt || 487 ||

dhanyo'haṃ kṛtakṛtyo'haṃ vimukto'haṃ bhavagrahāt |
nityānandasvarūpo'haṃ pūrṇo'haṃ tvadanugrahāt || 488 ||

asaṅgo'hamanaṅgo'hamaliṅgo'hamabhaṅguraḥ |
praśānto'hamananto'hamamalo'haṃ cirantanaḥ || 489 ||

akartāhamabhoktāhamavikāro'hamakriyaḥ |
śuddhabodhasvarūpo'haṃ kevalo'haṃ sadāśivaḥ || 490 ||

draṣṭuḥ śroturvaktuḥ karturbhokturvibhinna evāham |
nityanirantaraniṣkriyaniḥsīmāsaṅgapūrṇabodhātmā || 491 ||

nāhamidaṃ nāhamado'pyubhayoravabhāsakaṃ paraṃ śuddham |
bāhyābhyantaraśūnyaṃ pūrṇaṃ brahmādvitīyamevāham || 492 ||

nirupamamanāditattvaṃ tvamahamidamada iti kalpanādūram |
nityānandaikarasaṃ satyaṃ brahmādvitīyamevāham || 493 ||

nārāyaṇo'haṃ narakāntako'haṃ
purāntako'haṃ puruṣo'hamīśaḥ |
akhaṇḍabodho'hamaśeṣasākṣī
nirīśvaro'haṃ nirahaṃ ca nirmamaḥ || 494 ||

486 Salutation upon salutation to you, great guru, free from attachment, the embodiment of absolute Truth, with the nature of ever non-dual bliss, the sea of eternal compassion on earth.

487 Your very glance has soothed like gentle moonlight the weariness produced by the great heat of samsara, and I have immediately attained my own true everlasting home, the abode of imperishable glory and bliss.

488 Through your grace I am blessed, I have achieved the goal, I am freed from the bonds of samsara, I am eternal bliss by nature, and fulfilled.

489 I am free, I am bodiless, I am without sex and indestructible. I am at peace, I am infinite, without blemish and eternal.

490 I am not the doer and I am not the reaper of the consequences. I am unchanging and without activity. I am pure awareness by nature, I am perfect and forever blessed.

491 I am distinct from the seer, hearer, speaker, doer and experiencer. I am eternal, undivided, actionless, limitless, unattached—perfect awareness by nature.

492 I am neither this nor that, but the pure supreme reality which illuminates them both. I am God, the indivisible, devoid of inside and outside, complete.

493 I am uncomparable, beginningless Reality. I am far from such thoughts as "you", "me", and "this". I am eternal bliss, the Truth, the non-dual God himself.

494 I am Narayana, I am the slayer of Naraka and of Pura. I am the supreme Person and the Lord. I am indivisible awareness, the witness of everything. I have no master and I am without any sense of "me" and "mine".

sarveṣu bhūteṣvahameva saṃsthito
jñānātmanāntarbahirāśrayaḥ san |
bhoktā ca bhogyaṃ svayameva sarvaṃ
yadyatpṛthagdṛṣṭamidantayā purā || 495 ||

mayyakhaṇḍasukhāmbhodhau bahudhā viśvavīcayaḥ |
utpadyante vilīyante māyāmārutavibhramāt || 496 ||

sthulādibhāvā mayi kalpitā bhramād
āropitānusphuraṇena lokaiḥ |
kāle yathā kalpakavatsarāya
ṇartvādayo niṣkalanirvikalpe || 497 ||

āropitaṃ nāśrayadūṣakaṃ bhavet
kadāpi mūḍhairatidoṣadūṣitaiḥ |
nārdrikarotyūṣarabhūmibhāgaṃ
marīcikāvāri mahāpravāhaḥ || 498 ||

ākāśavallepavidūrago'haṃ
ādityavadbhāsyavilakṣaṇo'ham |
ahāryavannityaviniścalo'haṃ
ambhodhivatpāravivarjito'ham || 499 ||

na me dehena saṃbandho megheneva vihāyasaḥ |
ataḥ kuto me taddharmā jākratsvapnasuṣuptayaḥ || 500 ||

upādhirāyāti sa eva gacchati
sa eva karmāṇi karoti bhuṅkte |
sa eva jīryanmriyate sadāhaṃ
kulādrivanniścala eva saṃsthitaḥ || 501 ||

na me pravṛttirna ca me nivṛttiḥ
sadaikarūpasya niraṃśakasya |
ekātmako yo niviḍo nirantaro
vyomeva pūrṇaḥ sa kathaṃ nu ceṣṭate || 502 ||

puṇyāni pāpāni nirindriyasya
niścetaso nirvikṛterniräkṛteḥ |
kuto mamākhaṇḍasukhānubhūteḥ
brūte hyananvāgatamityapi śrutiḥ || 503 ||

495 I abide in all creatures, being the very knowledge which is their inner and outer support. I myself am the enjoyer and all enjoyment, in fact whatever I experienced before now.

496 In me who am the ocean of infinite joy the manifold waves of the universe arise and come to an end, impelled by the winds of Māyā.

497 Ideas like "material" are mistakenly imagined about me by people under the influence of their presuppositions, as are divisions of time like kalpas, years, half-years and seasons, dividing the indivisible and inconceivable..

498 The presuppositions of the severely deluded can never affect the underlying reality, just as the great torrent of a mirage flood cannot wet a desert land.

499 Like space, I am beyond contamination. Like the sun, I am distinct from the things illuminated. Like a mountain, I am always immovable. Like the ocean, I am boundless.

500 I am no more bound to the body than the sky is to a cloud, so how can I be affected by its states of waking, dreaming and deep sleep?

501 Imagined attributes added to one's true nature come and go. They create karma and experience its effects. They grow old and die, but I always remain immovable like mount Kudrali.

502 There is no outward turning nor turning back for me, who am always the same and indivisible. How can that perform actions which is single, of one nature, without parts and complete, like space?

503 How can there be good and bad deeds for me who am organless, mindless, changeless and formless, and experience only indivisible joy? The scriptures themselves declare "he is not affected".[33]

33 Brihadaranyaka Upanishad 4.3.22.

chāyayā spṛṣṭamuṣṇaṃ vā śītaṃ vā suṣṭhu duḥṣṭhu vā |
na spṛśatyeva yatkiṃcitpuruṣaṃ tadvilakṣaṇam || 504 ||

na sākṣiṇaṃ sākṣyadharmāḥ saṃspṛśanti vilakṣaṇam |
avikāramudāsīnaṃ gṛhadharmāḥ pradīpavat || 505 ||

raveryathā karmaṇi sākṣibhāvo
vanheryathā dāhaniyāmakatvam |
rajjoryathāropitavastusaṅgaḥ
tathaiva kūṭasthacidātmano me || 506 ||

kartāpi vā kārayitāpi nāhaṃ
bhoktāpi vā bhojayitāpi nāham |
draṣṭāpi vā darśayitāpi nāhaṃ
so'haṃ svayaṃjyotiranīdṛgātmā || 507 ||

calatyupādhau pratibimbalaulyam
aupādhikaṃ mūḍhadhiyo nayanti |
svabimbabhūtaṃ ravivadviniṣkriyaṃ
kartāsmi bhoktāsmi hato'smi heti || 508 ||

jale vāpi sthale vāpi luṭhatveṣa jaḍātmakaḥ |
nāhaṃ vilipye taddharmairghaṭadharmairnabho yathā || 509 ||

kartṛtvabhoktṛtvakhalatvamattatā
jaḍatvabaddhatvavimuktatādayaḥ |
buddhervikalpā na tu santi vastutaḥ
svasmin pare brahmaṇi kevale'dvaye || 510 ||

santu vikārāḥ prakṛterdaśadhā śatadhā sahasradhā vāpi |
kiṃ me'saṅgacitastairna ghanaḥ kvacidambaraṃ spṛśati || 511 ||

avyaktādisthūlaparyantametat
viśva yatrābhāsamātraṃ pratītam |
vyomaprakhyaṃ sūkṣmamādyantahīnaṃ
brahmādvaitaṃ yattadevāhamasmi || 512 ||

504 Heat or cold, the pleasant or the unpleasant coming into contact with a man's shadow in no way affect the man himself who is quite distinct from his shadow.

505 The qualities of things seen do not touch the seer, who is quite distinct from them, changeless and unaffected, just as household objects do not touch the lamp there.

506 Like the sun's mere witnessing of actions, like fire's non-involvement with the things it is burning, and like the relationship of a rope to the idea superimposed on it, so is the unchanging consciousness within me.

507 I neither do nor make things happen. I neither experience nor cause to experience. I neither see nor make others see. I am that supreme light without attributes.

508 When intervening factors[34] move, the ignorant ascribe the movement of the reflection to the object itself, like the sun which is actually immovable. They think "I am the doer", "I am the reaper of the consequences", and "Alas, I am being killed."

509 Whether my physical body falls into water or onto dry land, I am not dirtied by their qualities, just as space is not affected by the qualities of a jar it is in.

510 Such states as thinking oneself the doer or the reaper of the consequences, being wicked, drunk, stupid, bound or free are false assumptions of the understanding, and do not apply in reality to one's true self, the supreme, perfect and non-dual God.

511 Let there be tens of changes on the natural level, hundreds of changes, thousands of changes. What is that to me, who am unattached consciousness? The clouds never touch the sky.

512 I am that non-dual God, who like space is subtle and without beginning or end, and in whom all this from the unmanifest down to the material is displayed as no more than an appearance.

34 the water.

sarvādhāraṃ sarvavastuprakāśaṃ
sarvākāraṃ sarvagaṃ sarvaśūnyam |
nityaṃ śuddhaṃ niścalaṃ nirvikalpaṃ
brahmādvaitaṃ yattadevāhamasmi || 513 ||

yatpratyastāśeṣamāyāviśeṣaṃ
pratyagrūpaṃ pratyayāgamyamānam |
satyajñānānantamānandarūpaṃ
brahmādvaitaṃ yattadevāhamasmi || 514 ||

niṣkriyo'smyavikāro'smi
niṣkalo'smi nirākṛtiḥ |
nirvikalpo'smi nityo'smi
nirālambo'smi nirdvayaḥ || 515 ||

sarvātmako'haṃ sarvo'haṃ sarvātīto'hamadvayaḥ |
kevalākṣaṇḍabodho'hamānando'haṃ nirantaraḥ || 516 ||

svārājyasāmrājyavibhūtireṣā
bhavatkṛpāśrīmahimaprasādāt |
prāptā mayā śrīgurave mahātmane
namo namaste'stu punarnamo'stu || 517 ||

mahāsvapne māyākṛtajanijarāmṛtyugahane
bhramantaṃ kliśyantaṃ bahulataratāpairanudinam |
ahaṃkāravyāghravyathitamimamatyantakṛpayā
prabodhya prasvāpātparamavitavānmāmasi guro || 518 ||

namastasmai sadaikasmai kasmaicinmahase namaḥ |
yadetadviśvarūpeṇa rājate gururāja te || 519 ||

iti natamavalokya śiṣyavaryaṃ
samadhigatātmasukhaṃ prabuddhatattvam |
pramuditahṛdayaṃ sa deśikendraḥ
punaridamāha vacaḥ paraṃ mahātmā || 520 ||

513 I am that non-dual God who is eternal, pure, unmoving and imageless, the support of everything, the illuminator of all objects, manifest in all forms and all-pervading, and yet empty of everything.

514 I am that non-dual God who is infinite Truth, Knowledge and Bliss, who transcends the endless modifications of Māyā, who is one's own reality and to be experienced within.

515 I am actionless, changeless, partless, formless, imageless, endless and supportless—one without a second.

516 I am the reality in everything. I am everything and I am the non-dual beyond everything. I am perfect indivisible awareness and I am infinite bliss.

517 I have received this glory of the sovereignty over myself and over the world by the compassion of your grace, noble and great-souled guru. Salutation upon salutation to you, and again salutation.

518 You, my teacher, have my supreme saviour, waking me up from sleep through your infinite compassion, lost in a vast dream as I was and afflicted every day by countless troubles in the Māyā-created forest of birth, old age and death, and tormented by the tiger of this feeling myself the doer.

519 Salutation to you, King of gurus, who remain always the same in your greatness. Salutation to you who are manifest as all this that we see.

520 Seeing his noble disciple, who had achieved the joy of his true nature in samadhi, who had awaken to the Truth, and experienced deep inner contentment, kneeling thus before him, the best of teachers and supreme great soul spoke again and said these words.

brahmapratyayasantatirjagadato brahmaiva tatsarvataḥ
paśyādhyātmadṛśā praśāntamanasā sarvāsvavasthāsvapi |
rūpādanyadavekṣitaṃ kimabhitaścakṣuṣmatāṃ dṛśyate
tadvadbrahmavidaḥ sataḥ kimaparaṃ buddhervihārāspadam || 521 ||

kastāṃ parānandarasānubhūti
mṛtsṛjya śūnyeṣu rameta vidvān |
candre mahālhādini dīpyamāne
citrendumālokayituṃ ka icchet || 522 ||

asatpadārthānubhavena kiṃcin
na hyasti tṛptirna ca duḥkhahāniḥ |
tadadvayānandarasānubhūtyā
tṛptaḥ sukhaṃ tiṣṭha sadātmaniṣṭhayā || 523 ||

svameva sarvathā paśyanmanyamānaḥ svamadvayam |
svānandamanubhuñjānaḥ kālaṃ naya mahāmate || 524 ||

akhaṇḍabodhātmani nirvikalpe
vikalpanaṃ vyomni puraprakalpanam |
tadadvayānandamayātmanā sadā
śāntiṃ parāmetya bhajasva maunam || 525 ||

tūṣṇīmavasthā paramopaśāntiḥ
buddherasatkalpavikalpahetoḥ |
brahmātmana brahmavido mahātmano
yatrādvayānandasukhaṃ nirantaram || 526 ||

nāsti nirvāsanānmaunātparaṃ sukhakṛduttamam |
vijñātātmasvarūpasya svānandarasapāyinaḥ || 527 ||

gacchaṃstiṣṭhannupaviśañchayāno vānyathāpi vā |
yathecchayā vasedvidvānātnārāmaḥ sadā muniḥ || 528 ||

521 The world is a sequence of experiences of God, so it is God that is everything, and one should see this in all circumstances with inner insight and a peaceful mind. What has ever been seen by sighted people but forms, and in the same way what other resort is there for a man of understanding but to know God?

522 What man of wisdom would abandon the experience of supreme bliss to take pleasure in things with no substance? When the beautiful moon iself is shining, who would want to look at just a painted moon?

523 There is no satisfaction or elimination of suffering through the experience of unreal things, so experience that non-dual bliss and remain happily content established in to your own true nature.

524 Pass your time, noble one, in being aware of your true nature everywhere, thinking of yourself as non-dual, and enjoying the bliss inherent in yourself.

525 Imagining things about the unimaginable and indivisible nature of awareness is building castles in the sky, so transcending this, experience the supreme peace of silence through your true nature composed of that non-dual bliss.

526 The ultimate tranquillity is the return to silence of the intellect, since the intellect is the cause of false assumptions, and in this peace the great souled man who knows God and who has become God experiences the infinite joy of non-dual bliss.

527 For the man who has recognized his own nature and who is enjoying the experience of inner bliss, there is nothing that gives him greater satisfaction than the peace that comes from having no desires.

528 A wise and silent ascetic lives as he pleases finding his joy in himself at all times whether walking, standing, sitting, lying down or whatever.

na deśakālāsanadigyamādi
lakṣyādyapekṣāpratibaddhavṛtteḥ |
saṃsiddhatattvasya mahātmano'sti
svavedane kā niyamādyavasthā || 529 ||

ghaṭo'yamiti vijñātuṃ niyamaḥ ko'nvavekṣate |
vinā pramāṇasuṣṭhutvaṃ yasmin sati padārthadhīḥ || 530 ||

ayamātmā nityasiddhaḥ pramāṇe sati bhāsate |
na deśaṃ nāpi kālaṃ na śuddhiṃ vāpyapekṣate || 531 ||

devadatto'hamityetadvijñānaṃ nirapekṣakam |
tadvadbrahmavido'pyasya brahmāhamiti vedanam || 532 ||

bhānuneva jagatsarvaṃ bhāsate yasya tejasā |
anātmakamasattucchaṃ kiṃ nu tasyāvabhāsakam || 533 ||

vedaśāstrapurāṇāni bhūtāni sakalānyapi |
yenārthavanti taṃ kinnu vijñātāraṃ prakāśayet || 534 ||

eṣa svayaṃjyotiranantaśaktiḥ
ātmāprameyaḥ sakalānubhūtiḥ |
yameva vijñāya vimuktabandho
jayatyayaṃ brahmaviduttamottamaḥ || 535 |

na khidyate no viṣayaiḥ pramodate
na sajjate nāpi virajyate ca |
svasminsadā krīḍati nandati svayaṃ
nirantarānandarasena tṛptaḥ || 536 ||

kṣudhāṃ dehavyathāṃ tyaktvā bālaḥ krīḍati vastuniḥ |
tathaiva vidvān ramate nirmamo nirahaṃ sukhī || 537 ||

529 The great soul who has come to know the Truth and whose mental functions are not constrained has no concerns about such things as his aims in matters of locality, time, posture, direction and discipline etc. There can be no dependence on things like discipline when one knows oneself.

530 What discipline is required to recognize that "This is a jar"? All that is necessary is for the means of perception to be in good condition, and if they are, one recognizes the object.

531 In the same way this true nature of ours is obvious if the means of perception are present. It does not require a special place or time or purification.

532 There are no qualifications necessary to know one's own name, and the same is true for the knower of God's knowledge that "I am God.

533 How can something else, without substance, unreal and trivial, illuminate that by whose great radiance the whole world is illuminated?

534 What can illuminate that Knower by whom the Vedas, and other scriptures as well as all creatures themselves are given meaning?

535 This light is within us, infinite in power, our true nature, immeasurable and the common experience of all. When a man free from bonds comes to know it, this knower of God stands out supreme among the supreme.

536 He is neither upset nor pleased by the senses, nor is he attached to or averse to them, but his sport is always within and his enjoyment is in himself, satisfied with the enjoyment of infinite bliss.

537 A child plays with a toy ignoring hunger and physical discomfort, and in the same way a man of realization is happy and contented free from "me" and "mine".

cintāśūnyamadainyabhaikṣamaśanaṃ pānaṃ saridvāriṣu
svātantryeṇa niraṅkuśā sthitirabhīrnidrā śmaśāne vane |
vastraṃ kṣālanaśoṣaṇādirahitaṃ digvāstu śayyā mahī
saṃcāro nigamāntavīthiṣu vidāṃ krīḍā pare brahmaṇi || 538 ||

vimānamālambya śarīrametad
bhunaktyaśeṣānviṣayānupasthitān |
parecchayā bālavadātmavettā
yo'vyaktaliṅgo'nanuṣaktabāhyaḥ || 539 ||

digambaro vāpi ca sāmbaro vā
tvagambaro vāpi cidambarasthaḥ |
unmattavadvāpi ca bālavadvā
piśācavadvāpi caratyavanyām || 540 ||

kāmānniṣkāmarūpī saṃścaratyekacāro muniḥ |
svātmanaiva sadā tuṣṭaḥ svayaṃ sarvātmanā sthitaḥ || 541 ||

kvacinmūḍho vidvān kvacidapi mahārājavibhavaḥ
kvacidbhrāntaḥ saumyaḥ kvacidajagarācārakalitaḥ |
kvacitpātrībhūtaḥ kvacidavamataḥ kvāpyaviditaḥ
caratyevaṃ prājñaḥ satataparamānandasukhitaḥ || 542 ||

nirdhano'pi sadā tuṣṭo'pyasahāyo mahābalaḥ |
nityatṛpto'pyabhuñjāno'pyasamaḥ samadarśanaḥ || 543 ||

api kurvannakurvāṇaścābhoktā phalabhogyapi |
śarīryapyaśarīryeṣa paricchinno'pi sarvagaḥ || 544 ||

aśarīraṃ sadā santamimaṃ brahmavidaṃ kvacit |
priyāpriye na spṛśatastathaiva ca śubhāśubhe || 545 ||

538 Men of realization live free from preoccupation, eating food begged without humiliation, drinking the water of streams, living freely and without constraint, sleeping in cemetery or forest, their clothing space itself, which needs no care such as washing and drying, the earth as their bed, following the paths of the scriptures, and their sport in the supreme nature of God.

539 He who knows himself, wears no distinguishing mark and is unattached to the senses, and treats his body as a vehicle, experiencing the various objects as they present themselves like a child dependent on the wishes of others.

540 He who is clothed in knowledge roams the earth freely, whether dressed in space itself, properly dressed, or perhaps dressed in skins, and whether in appearance a madman, a child or a ghost.

541 The wise man lives as the embodiment of dispassion even amid passions, he travels alone even in company, he is always satisfied with his own true nature and established in himself as the self of all.

542 The wise man who is always enjoying supreme bliss lives like this—sometimes appearing a fool, sometimes a clever man, sometimes regal, sometimes mad, sometimes gentle, sometimes venomous, sometimes respected, sometimes despised, and sometimes simply unnoticed.

543 Even when poor always contented, even without assistance always strong, always satisfied even without eating, without equal, but looking on everything with an equal eye.

544 This man is not acting even when acting, experiences the fruits of past actions but is not the reaper of the consequences, with a body and yet without a body, prescribed and yet present everywhere.

545 Thoughts of pleasant and unpleasant as well as thoughts of good and bad do not touch this knower of God who has no body and who is always at peace.

sthūlādisaṃbandhavato'bhimāninaḥ
sukhaṃ ca duḥkhaṃ ca śubhāśubhe ca |
vidhvastabandhasya sadātmano muneḥ
kutaḥ śubhaṃ vāpyaśubhaṃ phalaṃ vā || 546 ||

tamasā grastavadbhānādagrasto'pi ravirjanaiḥ |
grasta ityucyate bhrāntyāṃ hyajñātvā vastulakṣaṇam || 547 ||

tadvaddehādibandhebhyo vimuktaṃ brahmavittamam |
paśyanti dehivanmūḍhāḥ śarīrābhāsadarśanāt || 548 ||

ahirnirlvayanīṃ vāyaṃ muktvā dehaṃ tu tiṣṭhati |
itastataścālyamāno yatkiṃcitprāṇavāyunā || 549 ||

strotasā nīyate dāru yathā nimnonnatasthalam |
daivena nīyate deho yathākālopabhuktiṣu || 550 ||

prārabdhakarmaparikalpitavāsanābhiḥ
saṃsārivaccarati bhuktiṣu muktadehaḥ |
siddhaḥ svayaṃ vasati sākṣivadatra tūṣṇīṃ
cakrasya mūlamiva kalpavikalpaśūnyaḥ || 551 ||

naivendriyāṇi viṣayeṣu niyuṅkta eṣa
naivāpayuṅkta updarśanalakṣaṇasthaḥ |
naiva kriyāphalamapīṣadavekṣate sa
svānandasāndrarasapānasumattacittaḥ || 552 ||

lakṣyālakṣyagatiṃ tyaktvā yastiṣṭhetkevalātmanā |
śiva eva svayaṃ sākṣādayaṃ brahmaviduttamaḥ || 553 ||

jīvanneva sadā muktaḥ kṛtārtho brahmavittamaḥ |
upādhināśādbrahmaiva san brahmāpyeti nirdvayam || 554 ||

546 Pleasure and pain and good and bad exist for him who identifies himself with ideas of a physical body and so on. How can there be good or bad consequences for the wise man who has brokened his bonds and is one with Reality?

547 The sun appears to be swallowed up by the darkness in an eclipse and is mistakenly called swallowed up by people through misunderstanding of the nature of things.

548 In the same way the ignorant, see even the greatest knower of God, though free from the bonds of the body and so on, as having a body since they can see what is obviously still a body.

549 Such a man remains free of the body, and moves here and there as impelled by the winds of energy, like a snake that has cast its skin.

550 Just as a piece of wood is carried high and low by a stream, so the body is carried along by causality as the appropriate fruits of past actions present themselves.

551 The man free from identification with the body lives experiencing the causal effects of previously entertained desires, just like the man subject to samsara, but, being realized, he remains silently within himself as the witness there, empty of further mental imaginations—like the axle of a wheel.

552 He whose mind is intoxicated with the drink of the pure bliss of self-knowledge does not turn the senses towards their objects, nor does he turn them away from them, but remains as a simple spectator, and regards the results of actions without the least concern.

553 He who has given up choosing one goal from another, and who remains perfect in himself as the spectator of his own good fortune—he is the supreme knower of God.

554 Liberated forever here and now, having achieved his purpose, the perfect knower of God, being God himself by the destruction of all false identifications, goes to the non-dual God.

śailūṣo veṣasadbhāvā bhāvayośca yathā pumān |
tathaiva brahmavicchreṣṭhaḥ sadā brahmaiva nāparaḥ || 555 ||

yatra kvāpi viśīrṇaṃ satparṇamiva tarorvapuḥ patatāt |
brahmībhūtasya yateḥ prāgeva taccidagninā dagdham || 556 ||

sadātmani brahmaṇi tiṣṭhato muneḥ
pūrṇādvayānandamayātmanā sadā |
na deśakālādyucitapratīkṣā
tvaṅmāṃsaviṭpiṇḍavisarjanāya || 557 ||

dehasya mokṣo no mokṣo na daṇḍasya kamaṇḍaloḥ |
avidyāhṛdayagranthimokṣo mokṣo yatastataḥ || 558 ||

kulyāyāmatha nadyāṃ vā śivakṣetre'pi catvare |
parṇaṃ patati cettena taroḥ kiṃ nu śubhāśubham || 559 ||

patrasya puṣpasya phalasya nāśavad
dehendriyaprāṇadhiyāṃ vināśaḥ |
naivātmanaḥ svasya sadātmakasyā
nandākṛtervṛkṣavadasti caiṣaḥ || 560 ||

prajñānaghana ityātmalakṣaṇaṃ satyasūcakam |
anūdyaupādhikasyaiva kathayanti vināśanam || 561 ||

avināśī vā are'yamātmeti śrutirātmanaḥ |
prabravītyavināśitvaṃ vinaśyatsu vikāriṣu || 562 ||

pāṣāṇavṛkṣatṛṇadhānyakaḍaṅkarādyā
dagdhā bhavanti hi mṛdeva yathā tathaiva |
dehendriyāsumana ādi samastadṛśyaṃ
jñānāgnidagdhamupayāti parātmabhāvam || 563 ||

555 Just as an actor, whatever his costume may or may not be, is still a man, so the best of men, the knower of God, is always God and nothing else.

556 Wherever the body may wither and fall like a tree leaf, that of the ascetic who has become God has already been cremated by the fire of the knowledge of Reality.

557 There are no considerations of place and time laid down with regard to relinquishing this mass of skin, flesh and filth for the wise man who is already forever established in God within himself as the perfect non-dual bliss of his own nature.

558 Liberation is not just getting rid of the body, nor of one's staff or bowl. Liberation is getting rid of all the knots of ignorance in the heart.

559 Whether a leaf falls into a gutter or a river, into a shrine or onto a crossroad, in what way is that good or bad for the tree?

560 The destruction of body, organs, vitality and intellect is like the destruction of a leaf, a flower or a fruit. It is not the destruction of oneself, but of something which is not the cause of happiness for one's true self. That remains like the tree.

561 The scriptures that teach the truth declare that the property of one's true nature is "a mass of intelligence",[35] and they talk of the destruction of secondary additional attributes only.

562 The scripture declares of the true self that "This Self is truly imperishable",[36] the indestructible reality in the midst of changing things subject to destruction.

563 In the same way that burnt stones, trees, grass, rice, straw, cloth and so on turn to earth, so what we see here in the form of body, organs, vitality, mind and so on when burned by the fire of knowledge take on the nature of God.

35 Brihadaranyaka Upanishad 4.5.13.

36 Brihadaranyaka Upanishad 4.5.14.

vilakṣaṇaṃ yathā dhvāntaṃ līyate bhānutejasi |
tathaiva sakalaṃ dṛśyaṃ brahmaṇi pravilīyate || 564 ||

ghaṭe naṣṭe yathā vyoma vyomaiva bhavati sphuṭam |
tathaivopādhivilaye brahmaiva brahmavitsvayam || 565 ||

kṣīraṃ kṣīre yathā kṣiptaṃ tailaṃ taile jalaṃ jale |
saṃyuktamekatāṃ yāti tathātmanyātmavinmuniḥ || 566 ||

evaṃ videhakaivalyaṃ sanmātratvamakhaṇḍitam |
brahmabhāvaṃ prapadyaiṣa yatirnāvartate punaḥ || 567 ||

sadātmaikatvavijñānadagdhāvidyādivarṣmaṇaḥ |
amuṣya brahmabhūtatvādbrahmaṇaḥ kuta udbhavaḥ || 568 ||

māyākḷptau bandhamokṣau na staḥ svātmani vastutaḥ |
yathā rajjau niṣkriyāyāṃ sarpābhāsavinirgamau || 569 ||

āvṛteḥ sadasattvābhyāṃ vaktavye bandhamokṣaṇe |
nāvṛtirbrahmaṇaḥ kācidanyābhāvādanāvṛtam
yadyastyadvaitahāniḥ syāddvaitaṃ no sahate śrutiḥ || 570 ||

bandhañca mokṣañca mṛṣaiva mūḍhā
buddherguṇaṃ vastuni kalpayanti |
dṛgāvṛtiṃ meghakṛtāṃ yathā ravau
yato'dvayāsaṅgacidetadakṣaram || 571 ||

astīti pratyayo yaśca yaśca nāstīti vastuni |
buddhereva guṇāvetau na tu nityasya vastunaḥ || 572 ||

atastau māyayā kḷptau bandhamokṣau na cātmani |
niṣkale niṣkriye śānte niravadye nirañjane
advitīye pare tattve vyomavatkalpanā kutaḥ || 573 ||

564 Just as darkness, though distinct from it, disappears in the light of the sun, so all that we can see disappears in God.

565 Just as when a jar is broken the space in it becomes manifest as space again, so the knower of God becomes the God in himself with the elimination of false identifications.

566 Like milk poured into milk, oil into oil and water into water, so the ascetic who knows himself becomes united with the One in himself.

567 The ascetic who has thus achieved the nature of God, perfectly free of the body and with the indivisible nature of Reality, does not come back again.

568 How could the brahmin come back again after becoming God when his external features of ignorance and so on have been burned by the recognition of his oneness with the Truth?

569 The Māyā-produced alternatives of bondage and liberation do not really exist in one's true nature, just as the alternatives of there being a snake or not do not exist in the rope which is not affected by them.

570 Bondage and liberation can be referred to only in connection with the existence or absence of something covering what is really there, but there can be no covering of God as there is nothing else and no covering, since this would destroy the non-duality of God, and the scriptures do not admit duality.

571 Bondage and liberation are unreal. They are an effect of the intellect which the stupid identify with reality just like the covering of the sight caused by a cloud is applied to the sun. For this imperishable Reality is non-dual, unattached and consciousness.

572 The opinion that this covering exists or does not exist in the underlying reality is an attribute of the intellect and not of the eternal reality underneath.

573 So these alternatives of bondage and liberation are produced by Māyā and not in one's true nature. How can there be the idea of them in the non-dual supreme Truth which is without parts, actionless, peaceful, indestructible, and without blemish, like space?

na nirodho na cotpattirna baddho na ca sādhakaḥ |
na mumukṣurna vai mukta ityeṣā paramārthatā || 574 ||

sakalanigamacūḍāsvāntasiddhāntarūpaṃ
paramidamatiguhyaṃ darśitaṃ te mayādya |
apagatakalidoṣaṃ kāmanirmuktabuddhiṃ
svasutavadasakṛttvāṃ bhāvyitvā mumukṣum || 575 ||

iti śrutvā gurorvākyaṃ praśrayeṇa kṛtānatiḥ |
sa tena samanujñāto yayau nirmuktabandhanaḥ || 576 ||

gurureva sadānandasindhau nirmagnamānasaḥ |
pāvayanvasudhāṃ sarvāṇvicacāra nirantaraḥ || 577 ||

ityācāryasya śiṣyasya saṃvādenātmalakṣaṇam |
nirūpitaṃ mumukṣūṇāṃ sukhabodhopapattaye || 578 ||

hitamidamupadeśamādriyantāṃ
vihitanirastasamastacittadoṣāḥ |
bhavasukhaviratāḥ praśāntacittāḥ
śrutirasikā yatayo mumukṣavo ye || 579 ||

saṃsārādhvani tāpabhānukiraṇaprodbhūtadāhavyathā
khinnānāṃ jalakāṅkṣayā marubhuvi bhrāntyā paribhrāmyatām |
atyāsannasudhāmbudhiṃ sukhakaraṃ brahmādvayaṃ darśayaty
eṣā śaṃkarabhāratī vijayate nirvāṇasaṃdāyinī || 580 ||

574 There is neither end nor beginning, no one in bondage and no aspirant, no one seeking liberation and no one free.[37] This is the supreme truth.

575 I have shown you today repeatedly, as my own son, this ultimate secret, the supreme crest of the scriptures and of the complete Vedanta, considering you one seeking liberation, free from the stains of this dark time, and with a mind free from sensuality.

576 On hearing these words of his guru the disciple prostrated himself before him and with his permission went away free from bondage.

577 The guru too with his mind immersed in the ocean of Truth and Bliss, and with his mind free of discriminations went on his way purifying the whole world.

578 In this way, in the form of a dialogue between teacher and pupil, the nature of one's true self has been taught for easy attainment of the joy of Realization by those seeking liberation.

579 May those ascetics who have removed all defilements of mind by the designated methods, whose minds are at peace and free from the pleasures of the world, and who delight in the scriptures, reverence this teaching.

580 For those who are suffering in samsara from the heat of the threefold forms of pain, and wandering in delusion in a desert thirsting for water, may these words of Shankara which secure nirvana and excel all others, procure for them the ocean of nectar close by in the form of the non-dual God.

37 Amritabindu Upanishad 10.

A Note on the Text

There is an anomaly in the text of which the translator John Richards made the following note, given in an appendix:

> The following verse is found in some editions, following verse 327, which also then omit verses 328 and 329. There are also other minor differences, above all in the division of the verses, but these make little difference in practice to the meaning.
>
> 328 He who has achieved perfection while still alive, is perfect when free from the body too. The Yajur Veda declares that he who sees duality experiences fear.

John didn't give the Sanskrit for this, but I have tried to determine the textual situation. John's main text is this:

328.1 tataḥ svarūpavibhraṃśo vibhraṣṭastu patatyadhaḥ |
328.2 patitasya vinā nāśaṃ punarnāroha īkṣyate || 328 ||

329.1 saṃkalpaṃ varjayettasmātsarvānarthasya kāraṇam |
329.2 jīvato yasya kaivalyaṃ videhe sa ca kevalaḥ
329.3 yatkiṃcitpaśyato bhedaṃ bhayaṃ brūte yajuḥśrutiḥ || 329 ||

328.1 From carelessness one turns aside from one's true nature, and he who turns aside from it slips downwards.
328.2 He who has thus fallen invariably comes to disaster, but is not seen to rise again.

329.1 So one should abandon the imagination which is the cause of all ills.
329.2 He has reached fulfilment who is completely dead while still alive.
329.3 The Yajur Veda declares there is still something to fear for anyone who still sees distinctions in things.

But John says that a two-line verse replaces both verses 328 and 329. I found only one reference to this issue at all, in an edition which gives the following:[38]

328.1 tataḥ svarūpavibhraṃśo vibhraṣṭastu patatyadhaḥ |
328.2 patitasya vinā nāśaṃ punarnāroha īkṣyate || 328 ||

329.1 saṃkalpaṃ varjayettasmātsarvānarthasya kāraṇam |
329.1.1 apathyāni hi vastūni vyādhigrasto yathotsṛje |
329.2 jīvato yasya kaivalyaṃ videhe sa ca kevalaḥ
329.3 yatkiṃcitpaśyato bhedaṃ bhayaṃ brūte yajuḥśrutiḥ || 329 ||

The edition also says (after 329.1.1) "extra verse number variation". I am grateful to my colleague Olivier Simon who has helped me with a translation for this extra line:

329.1 So one should abandon the imagination which is the cause of all ills.
329.1.1 Indeed I, devoured by disease, reject unsuited riches.
329.2 He has reached fulfilment who is completely dead while still alive.
329.3 The Yajur Veda declares there is still something to fear for anyone who still sees distinctions in things.

Based on this additional line, I cannot really reconcile John's replacement of the five lines of his main text with these two lines, which appear to be, more or less, alternate translations for 329.2 and 329.3:

328.1 He who has achieved perfection while still alive, is perfect when free from the body too.
328.2 The Yajur Veda declares that he who sees duality experiences fear.

The main text being the most generally accepted, however, we must for now let this remain a mystery.

Michael Everson

38 https://web.archive.org/web/20210506194245/https://sanskritdocuments.org/doc_z_misc_shankara/viveknew.pdf retrieved 2022-04-11.

www.ingramcontent.com/pod-product-compliance
Lightning Source LLC
LaVergne TN
LVHW011423080426
835512LV00005B/226